JUSTICE
FOR
YOUNG
WOMEN

JUSTICE
FOR
YOUNG
WOMEN

CLOSE-UP ON CRITICAL ISSUES

Edited by Sue Davidson
Introduction by Meda Chesney-Lind

National Female Advocacy Project
New Directions for Young Women
Tucson, Arizona

Library of Congress Cataloging in Publication Data
Main entry under title:

Justice for young women.

"This book is . . . a sequel to Teenage women in the juvenile justice system: changing values, published in 1979"—Pref.
Includes bibliographical references.
Contents: Listen to me: a female status offender's story / Debby Rosenberg and Carol Zimmerman—Domestication as reform / Barbara Brenzel—From benign neglect to malign attention / Meda Chesney-Lind —[etc.]
1. Delinquent girls—United States—Addresses, essays, lectures. 2. Female offenders—United States—Addresses, essays, lectures. 3. Sex discrimination in criminal justice administration—United States—Addresses, essays, lectures. I. Davidson, Sue, 1925-   . II. New Directions for Young Women, inc.

| HV6791.J87 | 364.3'6'0973 | 82-7848 |
| ISBN 0-9608696-0-3 | | AACR2 |

Grateful acknowledgement is made for permission to reprint the following material:

Barbara Brenzel, "Domestication as Reform: A Study of the Socialization of Wayward Girls, 1856-1905." Copyright © by President and Fellows of Harvard College. Originally published in *Harvard Educational Review,* May 1980.

Sue Davidson, "Advocacy for Teenage Women in the Justice System: One Model for Change." Copyright © by Associates for Youth Development, Inc. Excerpted from an article originally published in *New Designs for Youth Development,* Nov./Dec. 1981.

Prepared under Grant #80 JS 0020, from the Office of Juvenile Justice and Delinquency Prevention, Law Enforcement Assistance Administration, United States Department of Justice.

Points of view or opinions in this document are those of the authors and do not necessarily represent the official position or policies of the United States Department of Justice.

Table of Contents

Preface

This book is, in a number of important ways, a sequel to *Teenage Women in the Juvenile Justice System: Changing Values,* published in 1979. Like the present volume, *Teenage Women* was published by New Directions for Young Women, a service and advocacy agency for girls, located in Tuscon, Arizona. The book was meant to reach a broad audience with the special problems of securing justice in our society for those who are both young and female, and particularly those who are economically and socially disadvantaged. New Directions hoped to advance the status of these young women by stimulating improvements in day-to-day services, needed research, and organized action for institutional and social change.

Since the publication of *Teenage Women,* New Directions has continued to pursue the book's objectives, particularly through its undertaking of the National Female Advocacy Project. The advocacy project has produced and distributed sound information on young women and reasoned analysis of their condition— the required basis for any effective action aimed at meaningful change. The process is a circular one; for education is necessary to intelligent action, while action generates needs for additional information, thought, and understanding.

The selections in the present book are a rough reflection of that circular process. As Meda Chesney-Lind observes in the Introduction, the collection moves from factual evidence and description, to analysis, to theory, to the nuts-and-bolts of social action. None of these facets is isolated from the others; each is dependent upon the others. The process is not only circular but dynamic. Therefore, there is not only room, but urgent need, for the kind of effort represented by each of these selections.

This book could not have been assembled without the ready cooperation of the authors represented here. Thanks are due to all of them, not only for the generous contribution of their work, but for their willingness to meet deadlines that were frequently outrageous. The book also owes a very special debt to the director of the National Female Advocacy Project, Ruth Crow, for many valuable suggestions and for her support and guidance throughout. Others whose special contributions are acknowledged are the members of Work Shop Printers, Seattle, particularly Paul Atlas for the cover design; Rachel da Silva for the book design; and both of them for untiring technical advice on all aspects of the book's production.

It is not out of order to add here some final words of personal testimony. In Chesney-Lind's article on new research trends, she mentions the irony of a connection having been made in the popular mind between the rise of the women's movement and the reputed rise in female juvenile delinquency, in view of the helplessness and powerlessness of the young women typically drawn into the juvenile justice system. There is another layer of irony in the fact that among the activists, educators, and researchers in the women's movement of the 1970s, there was almost no awareness at all of the conditions of the youthful female offenders whose putative rebelliousness was being laid at the doors of the women's movement. I confess to having been among these ill-informed feminists, until I was invited by New Directions to a 1977 conference, to speak about books on women's lives and work in North American history. I went to teach, and stayed to learn. This book is for all who feel responsibility for society's most vulnerable members, and who will also stay to learn, to teach, to act.

SUE DAVIDSON

Introduction

Though it is often said that very little has been written about the female delinquent, this observation is not completely accurate. In point of fact, the books and articles, if piled one on top of the other, would make quite an impressive stack. Of course, what must be further observed is that the comparable stack of books on male delinquency (in most cases not prefaced by the word "male") would be much larger.

But what, over the last one hundred years, made the study of female delinquents relatively acceptable, when the study of women generally was almost unheard-of? Some answers to this puzzle can be found by examining the content of the writings themselves. Such an examination need not be confined to the dusty reaches of the library, either, since there has recently been a resurgence of interest in criminal and delinquent females.

This review would make it apparent that the study of deviant women serves important functions for the groups which hold power in society. Aside from the obvious need of these groups for intelligence about the characteristics of potential rebels, there is the undeniable fact that defiant underlings have always held a fascination for the master classes. As a consequence, long and detailed works on female law-breakers are welcome, so long as they ultimately warn other women of the terrible consequences of defiance, and stress the virtues and rewards of obedience. Most books on female delinquency and crime do precisely that. They accept female conformity as *ipso facto* good and incline to the view that any female defiance of authority will inevitably lead to a life of degredation, debauchery, and poverty. The authors of these works are generally quite eager to save women, particularly young ones, from this life of sin, and anxious to return them to their proper sphere — the family home.

The authors of most of these works, both the old and the new, tend to be very comfortable with maintaining the sexual *status quo.* Their insensitivity to the experience of women renders their works empty at best, and sexist at worst. The sexism of works on female deviants is often revealed not so much by what they say as by what they do not say. It is not unusual, for example, for the authors of works on female delinquency to overlook significant findings on the subject, even in their own data sets. In short, they have eyes but do not see.

It is the quality of most of the work on female delinquency that makes the present volume both different and important. Each of the contributions to this book turns a critical searchlight on the subject of women and society. In this strong light, the similarities between the experience of delinquent and non-delinquent women are often striking. The point emerges and re-emerges that women privileged and non-privileged are subject to contradictory cultural definitions, private demands, societal treatment. The contradictions in the position of the average young woman who runs afoul of the law are glaring: she is simultaneously a victim and an offender.

The links between the physical and sexual abuse of young women and their ultimate entry into the juvenile justice system are very clear for those who care to see them. Indeed, as shown by interviews collected by Debby Rosenberg and Carol Zimmerman, the young women are begging to be seen and heard. Says one desperate young status offender, a victim of repeated physical abuse and neglect, "One of these days I'm going to have to kill myself before you guys are gonna listen." Her story, frankly and poignantly conveyed in her own words, vividly sets the stage for the selections which follow it. She observes: "Males have it a lot easier in our society. . . . I got sent up to an institution because I was messing around. [My brother] went out and got some girl pregnant. He was only seventeen and he never got into any kind of trouble for it. She did, but he didn't. . . . That's just how it is."

That is not only just how it is, but as Barbara Brenzel's paper on the Lancaster School in Massachusetts demonstrates, that is how it has been, since the first reform school for girls was established in 1857. Using a variety of historical sources, Brenzel's work traces the relationship between the historic view of the female delinquent and the juvenile justice system's response to that view. Brenzel's research reveals the motivations of the early reformers, who felt that it was "sublime work to save a woman," because "in her bosom generations are embodied." If successfully "domesticated," she would become a docile housewife and mother. If left alone, however, she was a menace, for "in her hands, if perverted, the fate of innumerable men is held." This expression of concern neatly underlines another contradiction found in the study of female delinquency. On the one hand, the good woman, vessel of purity, was the guardian of moral and spiritual values, an example to her husband and offspring. On the other hand, the traditional status of all women was that of a piece of property. Thus a woman's private misbehavior has been perceived, and often judged and punished, as a property crime. In Napolean's immortal words, a woman is little more than a "womb with legs," the sexual property first of her family, and later of her husband. Defiance on her part, then, is inevitably evaluated with reference to her sex-object status. All her activities must be scrutinized with an eye on her sexual marketability (if she is young) and her sexual fidelity (if she is older). Consequently, virtually all youthful female misconduct is cause for anxiety that the young women may be led to sexual laxity. The solution lies in bringing her back into the family fold.

That solution to the problem of youthful female defiance, as Brenzel's work demonstrates, was one clearly adhered to by the reformers of the nineteenth century. Reform schools like Lancaster were intended to provide a "loving family circle" for the impoverished daughters of Irish Catholic immigrants, filling in for girls whose own families had failed to guide the errant back into the fold. Brenzel's work also traces the erosion of this benevolent attitude over the next fifty years, as Lancaster and schools like it became places of punishment and incarceration. The clientele remained, however, strikingly similar; over three-quarters of the girls had been accused of committing crimes considered "morally threatening to social stability." They were "stubborn," "wayward," "immoral" — the status offenders of their era.

The next selection, "From Benign Neglect to Malign Attention," covers some of the same historical ground in its effort to sort out the academic orientations toward female delinquency. The paper traces the role played by social workers and early criminologists in the development of myths about female delinquency and crime (such as the old notion that the justice system treats women "chivalrously," and the newer contention that the women's movement has caused an increase in women's delinquency and crime), and then demonstrates the important role that feminist scholars have played in rebutting these myths about the female offender and her treatment. This paper, as well as Brenzel's work, also explores the profound ironies in the justice system's response to youthful female offenders. While officials speak endlessly about protecting women, in practice young women offenders, most of whom come before the court for status offenses, are punished more harshly than their male counterparts, even those males charged with criminal acts.

The system's view of protection, however, is seldom one that is informed by consideration of the actual background of female delinquency. This background, both cultural and psychological, has been the subject of research by Debra Boyer and Jennifer James. Their paper makes a contribution by providing a comprehensive and non-judgmental analysis of girls involved in prostitution, as well as an incisive description of the process by which young women enter the street subculture which legitimizes their activities. It also reveals the role that sexual victimization plays in the young woman's transition from troubled adolescent, to runaway, to street-wise prostitute. But perhaps most importantly, the paper systematically examines those social patterns which encourage a young woman's drift into prostitution—for example, adolescent sex-role conditioning which leads young women to define their self-worth in sexual terms.

In "The Politics of Incest," Sandra Butler assails the carefully nurtured and self-contradictory myths which have allowed the crime of incest to flourish, while its victims kept silent, frequently blaming themselves for the assaults they suffered. She calls attention to the refusals of sexual theoreticians to recognize incest as widespread and common to all socio-economic classes. Additionally, she reviews the traditional clinical approach to incest, in which the victim is either not believed or held responsible for courting sexual violation, or in which responsibility is typically traced to the assailant's wife or mother. The acceptability of the pattern of "blaming the victim" also helps to explain why agencies of law are so willing to lock up young female victims of sexual assault (often in the name of "their own protection"), at the same time as they are over-eager "to believe the protestations of the immediately penitent aggressor." Butler's article confronts us implacably with the politics which support the oppression of young women as a class, but offers descriptions of promising programs and political counter-strategies for overcoming the abuse of children and women.

Additional information about successful strategies for organizing around issues of concern to young women is provided in Sue Davidson's "Advocacy for Teenage Women." Davidson describes the unique work of a handful of women in Tucson who, beginning as a miniscule force, have put together a national network of groups and individuals acting to improve the status of young women. While Tucson's New Directions for Young Women offers excellent and relevant direct services to girls, the agency also has a history of working simultaneously at system changes. When it received a modest federal grant to extend advocacy for young women to a national level, the agency's advocacy project set about to give other direct service providers a feminist outlook on the problems of youthful female offenders, at the same time insistently drawing the attention of feminists to the plight of these young women. The project has made an impressive beginning in persuading a diverse spectrum of organizations and individuals to work toward eliminating social and legal discrimination against young women.

Unhappily, at the very moment when economic misery is creating a potentially massive population of delinquents, public funding for projects such as that described by Davidson is being withdrawn. But because project members were well aware of characteristic fluctuations in the political climate of the country, they understood the importance of establishing decentralized forces and creating resources to assist them in their on-going work. Part of that task is the production of educational tools such as the present volume.

This book, then, is more than another reader on female delinquency; it may more properly be seen as an example of feminist praxis. That is, it first presents solid factual information on the history and condition of young women who are swept into the juvenile justice system, then provides analysis and theory springing from a feminist perspective, and finally explores ways of responding and acting that are consistent with that perspective. The work is both of the women's movement and for it and its supporters; and it is the authors' hope that it will prove useful in the effort to create a brighter future for the young women who are its subject.

MEDA CHESNEY-LIND
Honolulu, Hawaii
March 1982

JUSTICE FOR YOUNG WOMEN

Listen to Me
A Female Status Offender's Story

Debby Rosenberg
Carol Zimmerman

Introduction

Young women and young men come to the attention of the law *via* differing paths in our society and, once they are under control of juvenile authorities, they receive differential treatment. Contrary to popular belief, the law does not deal more gently with girls than with boys, but punishes them more severely for the same or lesser infractions. Behind these legal practices lie social convictions about the behavior appropriate to males and females, particularly in the area of sexuality. The situation is described with great clarity by Carol Warren, the seventeen-year-old status offender who tells her story here.

> I think that males have it easier in our society, even though things are getting a lot better for women. Boys do have it better, comparing my life to my brother's. I got sent up to an institution because I was messing around. He went out and got some girl pregnant. He was only seventeen and he never got into any kind of trouble for it. She did, but he didn't. If two teenagers get caught having sex, then of course it's the girl that gets arrested on an unlawful morals charge. What do they do to the guy? Nothing.
>
> It's just like in the family. If a man's daughter comes home and her hair's all messed up and her shirt's unbuttoned, he calls her a little slut. But if a boy comes

home and tells his dad he made it with someone tonight, he says, "Oh, that's good. That's my son."
That's just how it is.[1]

Under the guise of "protection," and "in their own best interest," the juvenile justice system subjects children of both sexes to a variety of abuses. Census data and independent surveys indicate that as many as half a million children are annually detained in jails—a figure the Children's Defense Fund characterizes as "grossly understated."[2] Nationally, an estimated one quarter of the children who come before the juvenile courts are not accused of criminal acts but of *status offenses:* acts which are illegal only if they are committed by a minor.[3] Young women are overwhelmingly processed by the courts for such offenses. Between 70 and 80 percent of the girls are detained for status offenses, compared with less than 25 percent of the boys.[4] For such noncriminal acts as disobeying parents, running away from school or home, sexual activity, and even as a result of being neglected or abandoned, girls are referred to the courts with greater frequency than boys, locked up more often and under more confining conditions, and kept under lock and key for longer periods.[5]

Like Carol Warren, a great many female status offenders are in conflict with their families. Most status offenders are referred to court by their parents, and females are more than twice as likely as males to be "turned in" by their own parents.[6] The pressures of a turbulent or abusive life at home may cause boys as well as girls to run away; but girls are more frequently apprehended and taken into custody. Following such episodes, if a decision is made that a girl is not to return to her home, there may begin a series of unsatisfactory "placements." Residential options and social services for girls, as compared with those for boys, are limited and often inferior. This is to be expected, in view of the infinitesimal public and private funds allocated to community-based programs for girls, relative to those for boys.[7] State "training schools" for girls—i.e., prisons—are in better supply. Available figures indicate that roughly half of the girls serving time in state reformatories are committed for status violations, in contrast to 17 percent of young men.[8]

The inequitable treatment of girls under law and by agencies of the law has gone virtually unrecognized and unacknowledged. This is the case even in the contemporary movement for children's rights and in the reforms begun under the impetus of the Juvenile Justice and Delinquency Prevention Act of 1974. Girls are generally invisible in official and unofficial reports and recommendations. It is only a handful of feminist scholars and activists who in recent years have begun to take notice of the double standard of justice which operates to penalize young women in statutes, courts, and correctional agencies.

Children as a group exercise no control over the social and legal conditions which govern their lives. The violence visited with impunity upon children, as upon women, is one indicator of their political powerlessness. "I'm really scared of my dad," Carol Warren says. "When I was little he used to knock me around." Adult women also suffer the violence of family members or friends in private, while outside the home the threat of rape operates as an informal means of social control for keeping women and girls alike "in their place." But women, if they do not hold great political power, at least by now have a long tradition of organizing themselves politically to struggle for their rights and welfare. Unlike children, who as a class are dependent upon adults to forward their interests, women over the past two centuries have increasingly come to speak on their own behalf. Children at the present time are without a voice. This is above all true of the sector from which the juvenile court population is drawn—low-income children, often of ethnic or racial minority background, whose interests are largely represented by middle-class adults.

When children speak about themselves, they give information which may be at odds with officially recorded statistics. Studies based on the self-reports of boys and girls, for example, reveal fewer differences in their "misbehavior" than courts typically yield. Not surprisingly, for example, although in some jurisdictions girls account for 100 percent of charges brought for sexual misconduct, the self-reports of adolescent boys suggest that they are at least as sexually active as girls.[9] More data gathered directly from young people are needed to document the ways in which sexist bias influences the juvenile justice system, ultimately benefitting neither the non-criminal young women who are unjustly punished, nor the society which they in no way endanger, either with respect to property or persons.

But statistical data, helpful as they may be, cannot render the human situation of individuals. In an effort to give young women an opportunity to speak of their own lives, in their own words and voices, staff members of New Directions for Young Women held interviews with fifty teenage women who were our clients in 1977. The experiences, thoughts, and feelings of these young women were valuable to us; and we believed that they might be valuable to others. The situations of these young women varied. Some came from group homes, foster homes, or detention centers; others came from a "normal home situation." Some had dropped out of high school because they were jobless, single parents, unable to pay for day care services which would have allowed them to remain in school, while others had dropped out because their schooling was not meeting their needs. Some who were currently in school had discovered useful classes and workshops at New Directions, such as those in job readiness or assertion training. Some came for counseling, which at New Directions is offered from a feminist perspective, geared to information, support, and guidance rather than to therapy. Carol Warren came to New Directions for study in the G.E.D. program,* but she also came because "you can feel comfortable here—get away from a lot of pressure and put your feet up." Others expressed similar reasons—"some kind of security," "someone that you could talk to." The young women, like the counseling staff, were from differing backgrounds—Anglo, Mexican American, Native American, Black—reflecting the major ethnic groups in the Tucson area.

Most of the young women felt some initial awkwardness in the presence of the tape recorder, but soon they were speaking openly and freely. The average length of the interviews was forty minutes. We covered selected topics: family, school, friends, drugs and alcohol, sexuality, career and life plans, social issues. Because our approach was topical rather than biographical, the interviews are for the most part fragmentary and do not yield sequential stories. With three of the young women, we were able to tape lengthy sessions, in which they presented histories of their lives. Carol Warren's story is one of these.

---

*General Educational Development—high school equivalency examination.

Listen to Me

I never knew my real mother. My parents got divorced when I was a year old and I lived with my grandparents 'till I was five. Then my father joined all these lonely hearts clubs when I was about four and a half and he got all these cards on people. There was this one woman in Florida and from her background and everything, my father thought she would be a good mother. They wrote two letters and they decided to get married. So he went down to Florida and she was in a mental hospital at the time, but the doctors said they wouldn't release her on her own. They said if she would get married to someone who was sane, who could maintain her and could help her take care of her, that, and spend a lot of time with her, that they would release her. They released her to my father's custody and they got married. We moved away and we never really had any problems. Then everything started happening at once.

My father told my new mother that he didn't want her to get pregnant because he didn't love her. He married her because he needed a mother for his two kids. But she got pregnant anyway. She refused to take her birth control pills. Then she had the baby and after she had the baby, she stopped even talking to me and my brother. She started kicking us around and busting us really bad, and then she'd put us down and say, "You guys are a bunch of fuckheads." She'd sit down there with her little daughter, hold her and praise her, saying, "You're the most beautiful thing in the whole world." We were always being put down, and that little kid was being built up.

They stayed married for nine years, but they got in big fights and she would leave. We'd be so happy and say to ourselves, please let them get a divorce. But it didn't happen that way. She'd leave a couple of weeks and dad would have a hard time taking care of us. So he'd write her and tell her, "I'll never do this again." He never even realized all those times she'd beat us. She put me in the hospital about five times. She put my brother in about five times, too. She seriously injured my eye when I was about six years old. Every time that she and my father got into an argument, it was our fault. What can a five- and a six-year-old kid do to cause that big of an argument? My dad is really violent. He tears things and he smashes things because he's got to get it out of him.

They had a fight and he left to go to work. I heard her in the room and she was beating my brother with the belt. I was scared because she really hurt me when she beat me. She wouldn't stop. I crawled between the bed and the dresser. I didn't think she could see me and then I looked up and she was standing over me and the belt buckle was hanging down. When she swung the belt buckle at me, that thing that goes in the hole went into my eye and it blinded me instantaneously. I was blind for a year.

She didn't call an ambulance right away or nothing. In fact, the whole thing, if I can remember. . . . She wasn't scared that I was hurt at all. The only thing that bothered her was that I was going to tell my father she had done it and she threatened me. She told me, "If you tell him that I did it, I'm going to kill you." Then she called the doctor about an hour later because I totally lost sight of this eye and then about five or ten minutes later I noticed that everything was really blurry in this eye and I couldn't see at all. The next thing I couldn't see. I kept telling her it's so dark, I can't see and she wouldn't let me go until she had made up this story and made me repeat it back about five times. Then she called an ambulance and I went to the hospital.

After they got a divorce my father got remarried to the lady he's married to now. My stepmother and I don't really have that good a relationship. I never really been able to accept her because she's a very insecure person and I believe the only reason she married my father was because she had two small children and she needed some security. My father represented that—just like he married her because I was fourteen and my brother was fifteen, and he wanted a mother for us, that's all. I didn't like her and I told him, "I'm not going to live in this house." I guess she really used to try to force me into trusting her and calling her mom and everything. I couldn't. She'd be so sweet to me, and I'd go into my room.

Her mother, from day one, the day she moved into the house, moved in with her. I hated her *guts*, you know, and she would put me down. She'd say, "Oh, you're so sweet," and I'd go back to my room and she'd go, "That little bitch, that little slut."

I used to get so mad, and it got to where me and step-mom would get into fights. But they weren't verbal fights, they were physical fights. She'd hit me and I'd hit her back. When I reach-ed fourteen, I decided once and for all that nobody was *ever* going to hit me again. After he divorced the first one, nobody was ever going to get away with it. So the first time she took a swing at me, I took a swing at her. Then I realized, when she told my dad, I had to barricade my door in my bedroom. My dad almost broke my door down and I decided there was no way I was going to be able to live there. So I took an overdose of pills and I just got real dizzy and I just passed out. I hit my head on the toilet and my mom heard and like she called my P.O.* And my mom had to break the door down because I had it locked. Then she pulled me out of there and I was uncon-scious and they took me to the hospital and pumped my stom-ach out.

They called my brother's psychologist and they put me in St. Mary's psychiatric unit and I was up there for two months. I told them, "You guys have to find a placement for me because I can't go back there." They wouldn't listen so they sent me home, and so two days later I took an overdose again. I told them, "You know, one of these days I'm going to have to kill myself before you guys are gonna listen to me. I can't stay at home." They took me up to St. Mary's and they examined me and everything and my parents were saying that I was mentally insane.

My parents just decided to take it into their own hands and they signed me into a mental hospital. They put me into Camel-back Mental Hospital in Phoenix for seven weeks and I guess I told myself, if they think you're insane, then you're insane. For the first four weeks I was there I was totally fucked up. Nobody could talk to me. I wouldn't talk to anybody. I wouldn't eat, you know, and I just made myself all weird out and insane.

Well, people could place their kids under CHAMPUS** if they could prove they needed it. So after seven weeks were up, my parents placed me in New Foundations. + I was there for three days. I don't believe that a program should be able to change a person's physical appearance just because they do

*Probation Officer
**Civilian Health and Medical Program of the Uniformed Services
+ A residential treatment facility, since closed.

something wrong. They caught me smoking dope. I had a joint and I was smoking it. My hair had been half way down my back, and it was my one thing in the whole world that I was pleased with because there was nothing about myself that I liked, except my hair. They cut it. They cut it off real short and they didn't style it or nothing. They just cut it straight off. When they did that I just said, "Forget it." I said, "Fine, you cut my hair and I know I can't fight you, but you can't make me stay after you cut my hair." They cut my hair and I went back to the place and I washed it and I left. I went back to the mental hospital and they took me to Juvie in Phoenix,* and they send me down to Tucson.

A place called Browndale** sent out some of their representatives down to interview me. It was the first time I'd ever had an interview that my step-mom came to. I had decided that I was finally going to deal with how I felt about her. I was going to be totally honest. I told her, you know. She was thinking of all these excuses and everything, and then she started yelling at me. She gets all these asthma attacks and she started laying this trip on me and my P.O. saying we brought on these attacks. I looked her right in the face and I said, "I refuse to accept the responsibility of your sickness and about these excuses, how it makes me feel. You know you don't give a fuck what happens to me. You really don't. That's why you're thinking of all these excuses. If you cared, you'd try to be here no matter what, 'cause I know if I had a daughter who was in a situation and I cared, I'd be down here through anything." Then my mother got all huffy-puffy and everything and she said, "Well, I thought we were going to court today." My P.O. said, "no" and she said, "fine," and she stood up and she walked out on me. It's like they say, the truth hurts. And for once, I told her really how I felt and I didn't say it violently or nothing. I was crying when I said it because it hurt, because I had to face that myself. It was one of the things I'd been striving for most of my life—to make my father proud of me—and it never seemed like he was. Finally it just seemed like he hated me. So why not fuck up? Why not make him hate me for a reason? It's better than nothing.

*Juvenile detention facility in Maricopa County, Arizona.
**A residential treatment center, since closed.

Then they decided to place me in Browndale. I was in Browndale for six months. I'd stayed pretty clean and everything from alcohol and stuff. Then I got a job, and I started really fucking up.

I had worked myself to where I was the most trusted person in my house at Browndale. I didn't have any set curfews. I didn't have to be there at any certain times of day. It was my decision when I was there, and when I wasn't. And they could accept it because I kept at the right times. But then I'd get paid and I'd be out all night. I'd come home at four or five o'clock in the morning. They couldn't have that, you know. Then they saw me driving and I was only fifteen. So they had to cut that out, too, and then they took all my privileges away from me. I could only go out just like everybody else, but I'd still go out and get drunk. So then they decided to put me on restriction, and took everything away from me because, they said, "You're messing up. You're fucking up. You're screwing up." I said, "Fine." So I went and had my friend buy me two lids and they brought it to the house. And I sat right there on the front porch and I got stoned and I told them, "You know, if you don't let me go down to the park and do it, I'll do it right here." Then they had a room search and they found it and they found my pipe. They threw it all away and everything. I got real pissed off and (sigh) I don't know, everything started happening. I had an argument with one of the relief counselors there and I told him, "I'm gonna take a walk because I gotta get away from here. I'm so mad I gotta get it out." And he told me, he threatened me, he actually said, "If you step outside this door, I'm going to call you in as a runaway." Then—I guess I'd never reached that point of being that mad again and I never had before—I just totally went out of my mind. I put my hands through the window and I cut the artery in my hand and I busted the window all over the place.

Then they put me in Americare Hospital, a mental hospital. I was in there for awhile and then they released me. The night they released me, the same relief staff at Browndale started putting pressure on me all over again, and I told him about three times, I said, "I can't handle this. I just got out of there. I've gotta slowly come back into things, you know. I've gotta keep my shit together." He just wouldn't get off my back, so I locked myself in my room and I started just throwing things. Then he decided, after he pushed me that far, he was gonna go stick me back in that hospital. . . .

They put me in a foster home. The people were real religious and everything. They were good people, but they could never understand other problems that I had. I stayed there about a month, and I ran away. I was gone for about six weeks and then I got caught. Then I went to juvenile detention. They gave me an examination and told me I was pregnant, which was exactly what I needed at sixteen years old. They had to decide what to do with me so they decided to send me to this place in Phoenix, a pregnant, unwed mothers' home.

I was there for about six weeks and I got in a fight with this girl. While we were fighting, she knocked me on the floor and she sat on me. Then I bled and I knew that I'd lost the baby, but I didn't say anything to anybody. I waited for about two more weeks and then I went to the doctor and he examined me. He told me, "You're just about as pregnant as I am," and I said, Fine."

I went home, and I packed my clothes, and I ran away again, because I knew if I wasn't pregnant, if I didn't have that excuse, I'd go to Patterdale.* Then I was living with my boyfriend down there for two or three months. And then my P.O. busted me one morning when I was asleep. They took me to Patterdale for sixteen months, and to Residential Intervention Center in Tucson.** That's where I am now.

*Residential correctional facility, since closed.
**Group home, since closed, affiliated with the Y.W.C.A.

Domestication as Reform
A Study of the Socialization of Wayward Girls, 1856-1905

Barbara Brenzel

In 1857, Bradford Peirce, superintendent of the first reform school for girls in North America, reported to the Massachusetts legislature on the role of female juvenile reform:

> It is sublime work to save a woman, for in her bosom generations are embodied, and in her hands, if perverted, the fate of innumerable men is held. The whole community, gentlemen, personally interested as they are in our success because the children of the virtuous must breathe the atmosphere exhaled by the vicious, will feel a lively sympathy for you, in your generous endeavors to redeem erring mothers of the next generation.[1]

Peirce was echoing a pervasive point of view in mid-nineteenth-century America, that in one form or another, social stability rested on women. Women would set the moral and religious tone for family life,[2] and family life itself would counterbalance the effect of unchecked economic change and the new extremes of urban wealth and poverty. Mid-century reformers had two solutions to the dilemmas created by capitalist modernization and its effect on the American family. One was formal schooling, which was a public and collective antidote to the disorder and chaos of the new urban environment. The other was the private family, which would offer—in a phrase recently reappropriated—a haven from the world of work and urban problems.[3]

The increasing stress on the importance of the family as a refuge crystallized expectations of women. Now they were to remain in the home, tending and educating the younger children while their spouses and older children left daily for the workplace. In addition to nurturing children, they were to create a sanctuary against the evil of the outside world. As a result of these expectations, nineteenth-century society become irreversibly dichotomised into the domestic sphere and the workplace. Obviously, poor women were frequently unable to fulfill the stereotype of true womanhood, for their lives were shaped by the need to survive rather than by social prescription. Nevertheless, this view of women — as social saviors guarding home, hearth, and family morality — continued to be the cultural norm and provided the model for social theorists and policy makers, as well as for women of all classes.

Poor girls were of particular concern to the reformers, who believed that rehabilitation of juvenile offenders was both possible and necessary. As industrialization, urbanization, and immigration surged, poor, deviant adults seemed less likely to be rehabilitated and assimilated into the new society. As optimism for rehabilitating adults waned, reformers transferred their enthusiasm for rehabilitation to children, whose innocence made them attractive candidates for reform. Children of the urban poor, potential street urchins, threatened social order; their future had to be engineered to preserve society. Reformers believed that these children could be re-formed at an early and still malleable age by giving them an acceptable type of family life. The dual motives of juvenile reform were to save the child and to preserve social order. These purposes were especially clear in the case of poor girls, who were considered potentially wayward — as vagrants and prostitutes. Saving the erring mothers of the next generation became vital.

In response to this pressing concern, reformers founded in 1856 the State Industrial School for Girls in Lancaster, Massachusetts. It was not only the first reform school of any kind for girls, but the first family-style institution in North America. Lancaster fused the twin nineteenth-century emphases on schools and families. Through the combination of schooling and reform, the girls at Lancaster would be saved so they could fill the appropriate female role within the family. Thus, reform ideology blended together the confused motives of benevolence and social control.

Once the school was established, it became apparent that reformist theories had to be adjusted to reality. Adhering to their belief in the family, reformers held steadfast in their efforts to train girls for the world of domesticity. The story of Lancaster is one of the changing definition of domesticity in the treatment of wayward girls. Although the school continued to train girls to fit into the domestic sphere, the emphasis narrowed from a total domesticity of surrogate family-style living and love, to an almost exclusive vocational training for domestic service.

What follows in this article is a social portrait of the reformers, the girls, and the school itself, in which we see vividly the expectations placed on women and changing but pervasive views of the role of domesticity. Studying Lancaster gives us access to fifty years of changing social theory about poor, wayward children, especially girls, and offers us a window on the past of the institutions we struggle to change today.

Methodology

Although historians have been interested in the lives of the poor and seemingly unimportant, they have found it exceedingly difficult to reconstruct the lives of the illiterate.[4] Until recently we assumed that many of the poor, especially poor women and children, had been lost to history. Now, material such as tax records, vital statistics, and census data as well as a more sophisticated use of computers has enabled social historians to write the history and to understand the lives of those previously forgotten. The Lancaster girls, the internal workings of the school, and reform thought are best understood by weaving quantitative and qualitative data together.

I have benefited from the new historiography and, by using the original handwritten case records, have gained rich and carefully detailed information for every entrant, for every fifth year for fifty years. By translating the data into a coding system, I marshalled certain facts about each girl: ethnicity, parental background, the family situation from which each girl entered Lancaster; her schooling, religious training, crime, complainant, behavior at the school, details of the indenture experience, and at least two "follow throughs," including place of residence and work subsequent to leaving the school. Many entries included a wealth of anecdotal materials about later events such as other employment, marriage, entrance into other institutions, or early death. I used indenture, employment, and place of residence to assess some of the school's outcomes.

Official statements made by the reformers of the day give us further information. Massachusetts state records contain many important discussions indicating attitudes toward crime, institutions, welfare, and causes of poverty and deviance. Legislative and other public documents of the Commonwealth, and early reports made by the Board of State Charities and Lancaster's trustees and superintendents contain much pertinent material. Some of the original diaries of the matrons and the budgets and personal records of the superintendent offer additional information. By concentrating on frequency distributions and cross tabulations, I have attempted to understand the interrelationships between all these variables.

The Establishment of Lancaster

Lancaster was an outgrowth of a widespread dialogue in Europe and North America that resulted in a series of institutionalized responses to capitalist modernization. As part of this ongoing transatlantic dialogue, state-appointed commissioners[5] went abroad to inspect institutions for juvenile reform. European reformers feared potential hordes of street urchins and, like their United States counterparts, combined a pressing need to control the urban poor with what they considered benevolent care for the deprived. The commissioners visited many schools, the most important of which included Das Rauhe Haus, Hamburg, Germany; Ecole Agricole, Mettray, France; and Royal Philanthropic, Surrey, England. These European schools espoused environmental theories of crime and vagrancy, and sought to counter detrimental environmental conditioning through family-style institutional life. Therefore, in all these institutions, dependent and deviant children were brought to live in home-like cottages in which they were to be treated with the firm but loving guidance of a supervising adult. The children were to live and be reformed within this surrogate family, as all were considered potentially salvageable.

The antiurban bias of most nineteenth-century social theorists was evident in juvenile reform. These schools were located in rural settings where children were considered safe from the evil influences of big-city life. The pastoral environment was believed to be purifying, a healthy retreat enabling children to redeem their lost innocence. A combination of religious training and family-style living within these rural sanctuaries was to insure that they would become reliable working adults and responsible family members.

Having studied these institutions carefully and discussed juvenile reform theories with European reformers, the Massachusetts commissioners returned to the United States convinced that family-style juvenile reform institutions were appropriate for the first American reform school for girls. Yet nineteenth-century Americans did not want to borrow blindly from the Old World. They wanted a New World version of the European reformatories and, in characteristic American fashion, placed great emphasis on education. The commissioners were determined, therefore, to draw heavily on those aspects of European juvenile reform that seemed most applicable to their mission. They embraced the family-style reform as perfect for the reformation of young girls; they envisioned that in the cottages of the heterogeneous reformatory, girls could receive the common schooling held so precious by the reformers and would acquire the habits of domesticity deemed critical for them. However, the reformers were also determined to avoid those aspects of European institutions that seemed too punitive, lacking in educational value, or inappropriate for women. They therefore rejected, for example, military routine, harsh punishment, and overemphasis on vocational training.

The commissioners returned to Massachusetts at an auspicious time. Nineteenth-century Americans were reacting to the crises of urbanization, modernization, and immigration by seeking to create institutions to mediate between older values and the consequences of modernization. Emerging cities with their large masses of poor and dislocated people, resulted in the loss of informal, familial, and community responsibility in which care for and control of the dependent and deviant traditionally occurred. Now, with towns swollen into cities, the same needy people were considered strangers; social reformers felt compelled to create new mechanisms to deal with them.

These reformers were, as a rule, driven by two motives: the hope of building a new social order, and the fear of social chaos. These motives were written into their reform innovations and characterized efforts to deal with strangers in their midst. It is important to note that Lancaster was an integral part of an institutional web[6] which had only partly begun to include reformatories, mental hosptials, public schools, orphanages, and various urban missions. In this light we can see Lancaster as part of an effort to care for and control the stranger—in this case, urban girls. This legacy was inherited from two sources: the egalitarian impulses which, in part, were inspired by the creation of America's democratic institutions and the common school movement.

The common school movement aptly illustrates the mixed motives of mid-century reform. Public schooling insured every child an equal education which would extend equality of opportunity to all children and teach them those habits of industry and morality considered important for responsible citizenship. By educating and socializing all children, reformers hoped to achieve social democracy and social order. Horace Mann, the father of the common school movement, articulated this dual purpose in his First Annual Report of 1837: "After the state shall have secured to all its children, that basis of knowledge and morality, which is indispensible to its own security; and after it shall have supplied them with the instruments of that individual prosperity, whose aggregates will constitute its own social prosperity; then they may be emancipated from its tutelage; each one to go whithersoever his well instructed mind shall determine."[7]

As a further effort to socialize and educate all children, the first state reform school for boys was opened in Westborough, Massachusetts, in 1847. Its purposes were to shelter those dependent and deviant boys who needed guidance beyond that offered by common schooling and to protect society from their potential evil. As Michael Katz discusses in *The Irony of Early School Reform,* a mechanism was created to educate and correctly socialize those who could not be reached by the regular process of common schooling.[8] In spite of the egalitarian rhetoric used to rationalize common schooling, however, the early reform school effort neglected girls. But the same view of children that led Horace Mann and others to promulgate common schooling for all children soon compelled reformers to offer the same reform opportunities to neglected and delinquent girls.[9] Mixed with this vision, however, was a growing concern that the family was faltering and the number of wayward girls was rising. It was, therefore, of immediate concern that girls, as future wives and mothers, be domesticated and reformed.

Given both their egalitarianism and commitment to common schooling, the reformers felt strongly that education had to be an integral part of the girls' reform program: they would learn to read and write as well as to perform household tasks and would receive rigorous religious training. Firm convictions of faith were motivational forces in the social activity of doing good for others less fortunate than oneself:

> Intellectual development exalts the moral, and although order and direct appliances may be necessary to complete its culture, still, when you open the avenues to knowledge and supply the mind with healthy food, it ceases to long after the garbage which works such mischief with those who have nothing else to feed on. The cultivation of *self-respect,* beside the inculcation and enforcement of those great moral truths which it is the business of society to develop and to cherish, should be carefully attended to.[10]

> The germ of all morality lies in self-respect; and, unless you have sufficiently stimulated and excited this, all your efforts will be as "sounding brass or a tinkling cymbal."[11]

The commissioners reported their thoughts in January, 1855 and in the same year the Massachusetts legislature established the school they wanted. The legislative resolves pulled together four critical aspects of this new social experiment. First, Lancaster was to be created and operated on state initiative. Second, this school was a manifestation of a larger enthusiasm for social reform. Third, the school was to be a great social invention, combining the best of common schooling with training in the habits of work. Fourth, its program orientation stressed meeting the unique needs of women. The Resolves expressed the theory which governed the creation of Lancaster:

> The title of the Resolves under which the commissioners act is, "Resolves for the establishment of a State Reform School for Girls." *A State Reform School for Girls!* Every word is significant and suggestive. In the first place the institution established is to be a *state* school. . . . Its establishment and maintenance will certainly affect the material interest of every citizen; and its beneficial operation will as certainly it is hoped return a manifold recom-

pense, purifying in its nature, into the bosom of society.

In the second place, it is to be a *reform* school. . . . Its aim to be the means, under the divine providence and by the divine blessing, of reconstructing . . . of rebuilding . . . or re-forming. . . .

In the next place, it is to be a reform *school*. It aims to accomplish its object in and upon its subject as *pupils*. It aims to enlighten the understanding, and to mend and regenerate the heart, by teaching the pupils what is true, and by training them to think and speak it, and by showing them what is good, and by leading them to act and do it. . . .

And, finally, it is to be a school for *girls*—for the gentler sex. . . . This circumstance is an important one, and enters into and modifies the plan of building and arrangement of rooms, with all the details relating to employment, instruction, and amusement, and, indeed, to every branch of domestic economy.[12]

The principle of in loco parentis assured the Commonwealth that the Lancaster girls were indeed to be treated as if they were under the supervision of a wise parent. The matron served as a mother; each girl was to have her own room, and no more than thirty girls were to live in the same house. In keeping with the staunch mid-century belief in the potential goodness of all children, the girls were not separated either by age or alleged crime. The older girls would set an example for their younger sisters; the younger girls would serve as gentling influences on the older girls. Corporal punishment was no longer an acceptable means of discipline; firmness and love stood in its stead. The girls would be bound in their new home by cords of love rather than imprisoned by bars.

Both European and American reformers were caught in a struggle between the utilitarianism most clearly defined in Benthamite ideology and the romantic view of lost community idealized by nineteenth-century poets, especially Samuel Coleridge.[13] While the utilitarians rationalized the growth and expedience of policies that resulted in the creation of social institutions and laissez-faire economic policies, the romantics yearned to recover the pure and pastoral. Lancaster was to provide the perfect environment to cleanse the girls, who were considered polluted by city life. The purity of natural living would inspire the redemption and healthy growth of the potentially wayward child.

Lancaster was nestled in hilly farmland in a beautiful rural area of Massachusetts about fifty miles west of Boston. A small stone chapel was built in the center of the grounds as a symbol of the school's mission. The girls' living quarters reflected the two goals of the founders. Each girl had her own room, although the size of the rooms and the layout of the sleeping quarters made them appear cell-like. Yet, there was pleasant common living and recreational space. Girls learned domestic skills in the ironing rooms in each cottage. In spite of this homelike atmosphere, however, the square, red brick building appeared less like the neighboring homes than the New England academies of the era. In this institution the girls were to be sheltered, educated, and gently incarcerated.

The daily life at the school was based originally on a balanced three-tiered program consisting of common schooling, religious observance, and domestic training. Life at the school can best be described by looking at the "First Annual Report of the Superintendent":

> The chapel bell rings at six, at which time or before, the girls rise, and put themselves and their sleeping rooms in order, and prepare the breakfast; at seven this meal is eaten. Housework is attended to until nine, at which time the chaplain comes, to take the direction of the morning devotions. Labor holds as many as can be spared from domestic duties in the workroom until dinner; this occurs at twelve. School is held from half-past one until half-past four; supper at five; and sewing, knitting and reading in the work-room until evening; prayers at eight, after which the girls are dismissed for bed. During the day sufficient time for exercise is allowed in the open air.[14]

Regardless of the age at which the girls entered Lancaster, at sixteen they were to be placed as indentured domestic servants. It was presumed that the moral and domestic training received at Lancaster would ensure that they were well suited for their placements. Girls served these indentures under the jurisdiction of the state until age eighteen, considered the age of majority. During their indentures, they performed household duties within a supportive and supervisory household.

The probate court was empowered to sentence to Lancaster those girls it felt would benefit from such a rehabilitative setting. Although they could be sent for both status offenses, such as vagrancy, and more serious adult crimes, such as assault, more than three-quarters of the girls had been accused of committing crimes considered morally threatening to social stability. For the full fifty years under consideration, most of the girls sent to Lancaster had been accused of stubborn, wayward, and potentially degenerate behavior; vagrancy, running away, and staying out late at night continued to be the most frequent female juvenile crimes.

Given the structure of the school, there could only be a small group of girls in residence at any one time. According to the Board of State Charities' Reports, the number of girls in the school averaged between 90 and 120. On the average, there were 69 entrants per year. It is important to note that the small group of girls who came to Lancaster had a great deal in common.

From 1856 to 1905, 75 percent of these girls were English-speaking, American-born, and very poor. Of the few who were foreign-born, almost all were Irish and therefore spoke English. Given the changes in immigration patterns around the turn of the century, it is not surprising that at that time a slightly larger proportion of the immigrant inmates were from non-English-speaking countries. Nevertheless, 85 percent of the girls still came from English-speaking countries, and the vast majority were native-born. A closer look at these girls' ethnic backgrounds indicates that most of them were the daughters of Irish Catholic parents. This is understandable, given the waves of immigration after the Irish potato famine of 1845. By the 1850s, more than half the population of Boston was foreign-born and most of these immigrants were poor Irish.[15] Therefore, it is safe to assume that their daughters were very poor indeed.

For these fifty years, Lancaster housed an almost equal number of Irish Catholic and Protestant American girls. It is considered unusual for such a large group of Catholics to be in a Protestant institution, except by force. Certainly by 1940, Catholics had issued public complaints against public schooling. In New York, for example, Catholic immigrants, through the efforts of Bishop Hughes, fought for public money to start their own schools. Catholic parents opposed the use of the King James version of the Bible, the lack of catechismal instruction in the classroom, as well as the Protestant insistence that schools be neutral. According to Carl Kaestle, many of the public school texts exacerbated this situation by containing anti-Irish slurs. In short,

Catholics considered the neutral stance of the public schools to be, in effect, Protestant and, therefore, anti-Catholic.[16]

During the fifty years studied, 6 percent of the inmates were black. Although this figure is disproportionately high when compared to the number of Blacks in the state at that time, the black population was steadily growing as black families migrated from the South. They, like the Irish, were poor and dislocated, but there is no evidence that they were selected to be brought to the school in any way different from the other girls.

It is also striking that Lancaster consistently housed children whose parents spoke English. Since the majority of the girls had been born in the United States, we may also assume that their parents had been in this country long enough to internalize the social norms, to speak the language of the probate court, and ultimately to make use of the system in order to find shelter for their daughters. Throughout these fifty years, more than half the girls, both Catholic and Protestant, were brought to the court by members of their own families. The complainant families seemed to have had in common a sense of desperation bred by poverty, unemployment, death, or physical uprooting.[17] That most of the complainants were family members undermines two popular assumptions: that reform schools were a malevolent plot of the state to take poor girls away from their families, and that Irish Catholic parents were extremely reluctant to place their children in a Protestant state institution.

Conventional wisdom assumed that state institutions, under the aegis of *parens patriae,* were legally sanctioned to take over child rearing because the natural parents were considered incapable. They were, therefore, considered enemies to families, especially to those destitute and foreign. Dickensian images of the heartless state hauling off weeping, protesting children from their humble, helpless parents are so ingrained that we are shocked to discover the extent of parental participation in a daughter's commitment to a state home.

As we have seen, Catholic parents exhibited great hostility toward institutions which they saw as undermining their own religious and ethnic identities. Understandably, their greatest hostility was directed toward schools and other institutions which cared for their young. Yet Catholics also brought their daughters to Lancaster.[18] It seemed that, when they were desperate, Lancaster was the only concrete help available to poor parents of difficult girls.

The evidence from the Lancaster School supports historians who consider most reform institutions as mechanisms for social control. However, the story of Lancaster suggests that our present understanding of the relationship between the state and the poor does not adequately account for the complicated web of relationships created among those involved. Given the benevolent impulses and the fears of the reformers, the seemingly inadequate supervision of the girls, and the desperation of poor parents, an inextricable triangular relationship emerged in the absence of any other welfare options. In large measure, the problem was the state's inability or unwillingness to offer more reasonable and less traumatic options for aid to the poor. Instead, parents were forced to take advantage of a punitive institution.

The story of Lancaster is not one of a dream come true. The Commissioners' lofty aspirations rapidly collided with social reality. In ways unanticipated by the reformers, the school had ties to social, political, economic, and institutional circumstances that would prevent it from becoming a rehabilitative utopia. Soon after Lancaster opened, the initial optimism of the trustees began to wane and, within a year, they began to doubt the feasibility of their scheme. Although the trustees continued to defend the innocence of childhood, their ambivalence grew, as demonstrated in the following passage:

> When the criminal desire has developed itself into the criminal act, the question is often asked, is there any prospect for permanent reformation? The answer will, of course, be greatly modified by the circumstances of age, previous social relations, strength of character, and their future position. In reference to the youngest cases, embracing even the astonishing premature age of twelve years, a glance upon their girlish faces will afford, in part, an answer to the question.[19]

The despair and frustration of the trustees and administrators was plain. Echoing the disillusionment expressed above, just slightly over a year later, another of Lancaster's trustees began to question heterogeneous groupings. He concerned himself with separating deviants from dependents. His rationale was a chilling harbinger of the policies to come. "This would enable us to separate those of a tender age from the older girls and to conduct, with a somewhat modified discipline, a department which might be considered *preventative,* anticipating temptation, and guarding the inmates from the peril of personal contact with the young offenders whose reformation is attempted in the other homes."[20]

By 1865 Lancaster was becoming less a place of loving familial guidance and more a place of punishment and incarceration. This was due to three interrelated factors: changes in reformist ideology, changes in the clientele, and changes in the school program itself. The Howe Sanborn Report, printed in the Annual Report of the Board of State Charities for 1865, indicated with frightening clarity the direction in which reform ideology was rapidly moving. The Report was concerned with the social burden of poor and deviant children and the elderly—those considered dependent. More important than this general concern, however, are the ideas found in the discussion of the "General Causes of the Existence of Dependents, Destructives, and the Like." Drunkenness was considered to reproduce weak stock, and there was also a strong suggestions of a new hereditarianism: evil tendencies were considered to be transmitted to children by parents inebriated at the time of conception. The report warned that the children of such a coupling could threaten social order.

Unlike the discussions of mid-century social theorists which blurred the distinctions between deviance and dependence in a sentimental judgment of all those who could and should be saved, less than fifteen years later analysis focused on the various causes of deviance. The concern shifted from saving children to classifying types of depravity. Although the authors of the report claimed to be confused about who was blighted irreversibly and who was redeemable, they revealed their hereditarian bias when they attempted to explain the difference between "lack of vital force" and "inherited tendencies." Mid-nineteenth century social theories had attributed juvenile dependency and deviance to poor environment and inadequate parents. Now the blame fell increasingly on the child, to whom the bad habits of parents had been directly transmitted.

At the same time that reform ideology was evolving toward a sterner hereditarian explanation for deviance, the age and supposed character of entrants also changed. Initially, girls between ages seven and sixteen were to be admitted to Lancaster.

However, from its opening in 1856, most girls were pubescent—between fourteen and fifteen. The age of entrants steadily increased, so that by 1875 most of the entrants were between the ages of fifteen and sixteen and by 1895, they were between sixteen and seventeen.

The contrast between the sentimental attitudes of mid-century reformers, especially toward younger girls, and the harsher attitudes later in the century are reflected in the superintendents' reports. For example, both Sarah W. (1856) and Elizabeth B. (1880) were sent to Lancaster as "stubborn" girls, on the verge of deviance, but supposedly redeemable. However, the tone of Superintendent Bradford Peirce, writing in 1856, differs radically from that of Superintendent Marcus Ames, writing in 1880.

Sarah W., brought in for uncontrollable masturbation, was described as a "pretty little girl . . . who would be a substantial comfort to anyone who would carefully train her. . . ."[21] Once it was discovered that she was suffering from erysipelas, a skin disease, rather than a need to "abuse herself," the state chose to keep her and thus be guaranteed that she would be properly trained. Bradford Peirce went on to describe her as "requiring medical attention and physical treatment."[22] It was unlikely that Sarah and girls like her would be considered incorrigible in 1856.

By 1880, however, girls were more likely to be described as Elizabeth B.: "Young as Lizzie is, her record is painfully bad. She has been off with bad men and to disreputable places on Charles Street."[23] Similarly, Winnifred C. is "unmanageable and disobedient; has been in bad company; appears hardened and utterly devoid of feeling or shame."[24] Certainly by 1890, Bradford Peirce's sensitive belief that the young "sinner" was to be pitied, loved, and redirected to a good life was replaced by that colder tone reserved for management of the unruly and depraved. The case report of Josephine C., the 1,557th entrant, reflected the officer's attitude toward newcomers to Lancaster: "[She] is said to be unchaste. Has not frequented houses of ill fame. She is not of average intelligence. Character of house not good. Father a drinking fiddler and her mother is deaf and dumb. Girl is on street. Stole a hat from a store in Holyoke. Her appearance indicates a want of teaching."[25]

This unfeeling tone colored reports for the next fifteen years. In 1905 the punitive voice of the superintendent can be heard in the description of Annie Elizabeth H.: "[She] is known to have been unchaste. Keeps low company. Out late at night. Character of home poor. Fa[ther] in H[ouse] of C[orrection] for drunkenness. Mother washes. These girls were found in a freight car with men. She has been immoral for some time."[26]

The Legislative Reports also systematically noted that the girls were harder and of a more "criminal" class, and now defined "criminality" in specifically female terms. The crimes reported at the boys' reformatory at Westborough were crimes which implied greater violence, and more damage to personal or public property. The more severe crimes for girls were those which suggested immorality, defined by wantonness and prostitution. No longer considered vulnerable to exploitation, girls now could be destructive of public morality. They were no longer seen as girls in need of protection or firmer, more loving supervision, but as threats to public safety in need of isolation and control.

The increase in the age of entrants, however, was affected by three legislated changes as well as by the emergence of new state reform institutions.[27] In 1871 the state passed a law which enabled the Board of State Charities to attend probate court and prevent younger and seemingly more innocent girls from going to Lancaster. The state could now intervene to separate the younger from older girls. This view countered the founders' conception of the family institution as a therapeutic environment. It was now important to save young girls from the potential harm resulting from exposure to older and more hardened girls. State policy now facilitated direct placement to help the young; direct placement was seen as less desirable for older girls. In 1871 other laws influenced the age composition at Lancaster. One determined that seventeen-year-olds could be sent to Lancaster. Another provided that girls of sixteen who were considered incorrigible or badly placed originally could be transferred to Lancaster from other institutions by the courts. Lancaster was rapidly becoming a dumping ground for older and tougher girls.

In 1886 the State Primary School at Monson opened.[28] The express purpose of this school was to care for young, destitute children. Younger girls who were originally to be sent to Lancaster were now to be sent to the Primary School. Although the Primary School closed in 1895, the age patterns at Lancaster remained relatively unchanged after that time.

While the original reform ideology of heterogeneous family-style life was debated until 1885, policy pressures and the working of the institutional web brought about the separation of younger from older girls long before the formal change in reform theory occurred. Segregation by age and character replaced the therapeutic vision of mid-century environmentalists and underlined an insistence on the permanence of taint. The state, through legislation, voiced its disbelief in the possibility of reclaiming innocence for everyone. It is difficult to evaluate the criminal character of these older girls, to determine whether they were, in fact, as the officers described them, harder. It is possible that they were more sexually experienced if only because they were older.

With the changes in age and supposed criminality of its clientele, Lancaster officials were forced to face pressing questions of management and control. Although, by 1877, hardened girls were being sent to Sherborn Reformatory for Women, an institution for adult female first offenders, the trustees of Lancaster felt that the increased number of hardened girls created a need for the school to have its own correctional department. The policy of transferring incorrigible girls to Sherborn sufficed when transfer was not a frequent necessity. By the 1880s, however, this policy was inadequate to handle the new clientele. The mid-century belief that "cords of love are stronger than chains of iron" and that "affection and attachment are more irresistible bulwarks than stone walls . . . that iron and stone may restrain and confine the vicious, but they possess no healing properties for the morally diseased,"[29] was now undermined by the request for a more correctional measure. "Isolation or separate confinement, with or without work, as the case may require, is conceded to be one of the most effective methods of bringing to a sense of duty the insubordinate."[30]

With the new institutions for the very young and channels for shipping off the unsuitable, Lancaster assumed a new role. In 1885, the trustees stated that "the Industrial School occupied a position more important than many it has held since its establishment. It is now a middle place between the care of the Board of State Charities and a Reformatory Prison."[31] "The inmates are lodged in four separate family houses, each with its own staff of officers. This division allows a careful classification within the school, a classification depending upon the character and previous history of the girls, and not upon age or conduct within the institution. As there is no promotion from house to house, a perfect isolation is thus secured of those who might otherwise contaminate the more innocent."[32]

A system to guarantee separation of girls by age and character was now in full operation at Lancaster. This classification system formally acknowledge the acceptance of the hereditarian argument for the causes of dependence and deviance. Older girls were considered more tainted, harder, and less redeemable. Hereditarians argued that most delinquent poor children suffered the "permanence of taint." In spite of this harsh argument, some commitment to the ideas linking childhood and salvation continued. Hope for some rehabilitation, therefore, was reserved, but only for the very young. The classification system also formally sanctioned a more punitive approach to older girls whose characters were flawed. Girls would now be treated as cases, rather than as souls to be redeemed. The work at Lancaster was to manage this classified system, making sure that the girls were appropriately placed in the school. The loving family circle was a forgotten dream.

Given all the factors influencing Lancaster's program—economic shifts, changing social theory, different clientele, and internal school pressures—the school's officials kept struggling to redesign a program suitable for both the social climate and the entrants. Therefore, the appropriate roles of common schooling, domestic training, and placement were constantly debated. The success of Lancaster's program had depended upon its healthy balance of religion, common schooling, and domestic training. This internal program was to culminate in a successful indenture —one where the girls were to perform satisfactorily as decent and self-respecting domestic servants. The indenture period was the most vulnerable part of the program because it depended upon successful training at Lancaster and a welcoming climate and job market outside the school. Flaws in the indenture system frequently resulted in efforts to redesign the school's training program and educational curriculum. For example, in 1868 the program was revised to include instruction in a wider variety of housekeeping skills to improve the capacity for housework. The trustees saw in such increased versatility a greater guarantee to the girls that "[they would] readily find safe and respectable homes, liberal wages and kind friends.''[33]

Although domesticity was always the prime objective of Lancaster's program, the increased stress on domestic training was now explicitly stated and justified as that aspect of Lancaster's program most relevant to the attainment of true womanhood. The details of this report read as a prescription for the happy lives of women:

> Almost every woman is destined to have a leading or subordinate part in the management of a family. Preparation for the ready and intelligent performance of household duties, the lowest as well as the highest, is therefore, of the first importance. Now, as perfect cleanliness is essential to health of body and of mind and to cheerfulness, all the arts of washing and scouring should be early learnt and practised, so as to form and fix the habit of doing them well, thoroughly, rapidly, and willingly.[34]

The report then goes on to list explicitly the chores most closely linked to those deemed essential for women's happiness: ''. . . these arts should include not only the washing of tables and dishes, but the scouring of floors, stairs, windows and walls, and of clothes, and especially of bedclothes, and bedsteads. These duties occur every day in every family. They should, therefore, be done methodically, and the habit of method and order should be insisted amongst the most important attainments.''[35]

Common schooling, originally seen as an essential feature of Lancaster's program, became less important as the push for domestic science increased. By 1869 education at Lancaster largely had come to mean female vocational training. The zeal of Samuel Gridley Howe and Horace Mann for common schooling was swept under the carpet with domestic training.

In spite of the newly tailored curriculum, by 1875 the indenture system was in even greater danger. The number of indentures experienced by each girl had risen, so that as many as 15 percent of those girls who were indentured had more than three placements and a few had as many as five. It seemed that many Lancaster girls were not suitable for placement and that the school would have to refine its program in order to increase the girls' employability.[36]

By 1884 the program had diverged dramatically from its original plan. The 29th Annual Report discussed the constant change of inmates due to a new policy which placed out girls as soon as they seemed ready rather than when they reached sixteen. This new policy left more openings for new girls, and since the average length of confinement was short, the whole idea of family-style care was undermined; Lancaster became less a residence and place for reformation and more a place for expedient detention.

Because many of the girls were at Lancaster for only a short while, the trustees feared that the school would become a mere custodial institution. Therefore, they decided to speed up their training and enable the girls to earn a living within a domestic situation. If they did not comply, they were punished by being transferred to Sherborn Reformatory.

In one sense, the trustees' decision made sense; training for service all but insured the Lancaster girls' employment. While employment opportunities for women expanded in the last two decades of the nineteenth century, domestic service continued to be the most available job for young women. In fact, the demand for domestic service increased as fewer women found jobs in service appealing. Many young women preferred to work in the mills and factories, away from the constant surveillance of the female employer. Moreover, many older immigrant and black women previously forced to live in as domestics preferred to live out and combine motherhood and work.[37] Given this demand, it is not surprising that the reformers chose to train Lancaster girls for domestic service. Not only was there a guaranteed market, but domestic service also continued the close and constant familial supervision of Lancaster. In many ways, the domestication of Lancaster girls continued beyond the school into domestic employment. This labor need continued well into the 1920s.

Regardless of this demand for domestics, several factors complicated the hiring of young women. One was that the marriage age had risen so that many young people remained at home longer. Given that more women had older daughters at home, it is possible that female heads of households would have been unwilling to have a non-American girl in the house. As Marcus Ames suggested, these women were no longer filled with mid-century benevolence; they were not anxious to extend their hospitality to the likes of a Lancaster girl. Rather, they wanted efficient and thorough work from their domestic employees. In addition, it seems likely that mothers might worry about the potential promiscuity between their older sons still at home, and young girls; any act which led to their stay in reform school was assumed to be evidence of previous promiscuity. Given the availability of jobs for Lancaster girls in domestic service as well as the bias of employees against girls who were untrained or in need of nurturance, the new policy seemed sensible. The affectionate domestic life of mid-century Lancaster became an artifact; in its stead was an expedient vocational training program.

The trustees recognized that Lancaster had become a school solely for rapid vocational training. The school was free of its mid-century conflicts; no longer did it claim to protect and reform deprived girls. Common schooling, once considered a critically important factor in the reformation of young girls, was no longer considered essential. Lancaster was finally adopting the type of British vocational program it had previously scorned. The shift in program, however, was part of a wider educational trend in which formal industrial education sought to prepare the poor and immigrant for jobs in the new industrial world.[38] At the same time, it was assumed that learning technical skills would train the whole child, that she would learn strong moral values as well as skills, and therefore be prepared to participate in the broader social world. Like common schooling, Lancaster's original program was no longer appealing.

Employment and Family Life

What impact did Lancaster have on the adult lives of its inmates? In keeping with nineteenth-century expectations for women, Lancaster girls were to live domestic, industrious, and morally upright lives. Although the founders did not anticipate that the girls would rise above their station, they hoped that they would live respectably.

After leaving the supervision of the state, most Lancaster girls continued to live as the founders had hoped. Between 1856 and 1905, 75.6 percent of the girls lived with a family: parental, conjugal, in placement, or in Lancaster itself. From this group, 35 percent returned to their parents. The pattern emerging from these first follow-ups continued. Most girls remained within a family environment, usually with husbands in homes of their own. There continued to be a small number of girls living and working alone, but there was little to indicate that the majority of them were living dissolute lives.

It is dangerous to assume a cause-and-effect relationship between Lancaster's program and the subsequent lives of the girls. Lancaster may have provided no more than shelter for poor and difficult girls; it may have been little more than a way station for them. Or it may have functioned primarily as a job placement service. It is also likely that it offered slight comfort to some parents skidding from the lower class to the underclass.[39] Perhaps Lancaster prevented this fall for their daughters and returned them to society as poor but respectable women.

The inherent nature of women was presumed to be domestic. Lancaster's program was designed according to this stereotype and offered what was "natural" for the reformation of poor girls. The environmentalists blamed poverty and slum life for the unrestrained, and therefore unwomanly, behavior of the girls. Later, the hereditarians blamed vicious parents, especially mothers, for raising "unnatural" and tainted daughters. The definition of "natural" changed from a state of externally induced conditions to internal character weaknesses. Lancaster's job continued to be the domestication of girls so that they would be better able to fulfill their "natural" roles; regardless of changes in clientele or social theory, Lancaster's main objective did not change.

Conclusions

The story of Lancaster, its goals and program, tells us as much about the nineteenth-century view of women's roles in society as about the institution itself. Lancaster's primary objective was to domesticate girls who were considered potential deviants. In keeping with contemporary attitudes, it was especially important that women, as potential wives and mothers, be respectable, morally upright, and industrious.

Seemingly seductive women had always been feared and shunned as dangerous, uncontrolled, and lascivious. Now, renewed pressure to secure the family increased society's expectations of women. They were expected to insure social order, especially at a time when there seemed to be precious little of it. Lancaster's program, although initially claiming a great belief in the role of common schooling as crucial to reformation, increasingly became a domestic training program. Regardless of these changes, however, most of the girls left Lancaster to lead lives of domestic respectability. Although the ideology of reformation degenerated into little more than rhetoric, the school seemed successful because there was little evidence that Lancaster girls ended up in jail or on the streets. This program, however, perpetuated the class structure that was a major factor in the poverty of the girls' families. Few rose above their station and few skidded to the underclass or resorted to prostitution.

It is most important to remember that there were almost no options for poor parents. The story of Lancaster, therefore, is not just about a reform school, but also a drama about the devastating effects upon families of poverty and public charity. The story of Lancaster also offers an overarching view of reformers. In the fifty years covered by this study, the initial exuberance and optimism of the founders abruptly ended. In their stead came fatigue, disillusionment, pessimism, and anger. The early optimism of the founders changed partly because of changes in clientele, and partly because of economic changes and shifting trends in nineteenth-century social theories. In the end, we are left with many questions about the potential success of any social experiment over time. The trustees and state officials did not remain sensitive to Lancaster's success as a reform experiment, created from policies which attempted to accomodate the inherent ambivalence of the reformers—fear and benevolence. In an attempt to create a social institution that would protect and guide children, as well as incarcerate them for the public safety, the founders of Lancaster created an institutional experiment based on confused purposes. The school was to make restitution for the children's deprived family lives by offering them compulsory love.

Lancaster's story is a gloomy one, a tale of the decline of hopes for reform into a desire for social control. There is sufficient evidence that the institutional attempt to counter the unchecked forces of economic and technical change was not by itself sufficient. However, the story is not simply a revisionist parable of an elite imposing its will on the passive masses. It is a story of true mixed feelings and mixed results.

In 1980 historians, sociologists, and social policy analysts are questioning the beginnings of compulsory school attendance, and the growth of policies that have given the state increased jurisdiction over the lives of children, particularly those who are seen as receiving inadequate care from their families. These policies grew partly as a response to the needs of poor and potentially delinquent children in the nineteenth century and have ultimately touched the lives of all children. They are particularly relevant to policy makers currently in the process of formulating new programs for juveniles.

Today, we continue to face heartbreaking facts about the treatment of female delinquents. While the story of Lancaster is not totally unique either to the Commonwealth or to girls, parts of its history threaten to be repeated, especially in the new programs for the treatment of female juveniles. In 1973 Massachusetts took great pride in its bold and controversial policy to deinstitutionalize children. Soon after, the boys school at Westborough was closed amidst an almost celebratory event in which a cavalcade of cars and vans from the University of Massachusetts at Amherst "rescued" the last thirty-five inhabitants of the school. However, Lancaster remained partially occupied until 1976. Once again girls were neglected.[40] This suggests that, one hundred and twenty years later, fear still exists; the story of girls at Lancaster threatens to come full circle. Nevertheless, attempts are now being made to avoid some of the mistakes we have seen in Lancaster's history. It is hoped that the story of Lancaster, and similar institutions, will prove valuable so that we can learn from the glaring errors of the past.

From Benign Neglect t(
Malign Attention
A Critical Review of Recent Research on Female Delinquency

Meda Chesney-Lind

For many years, it was not unusual for entire books on crime and delinquency to be written without once mentioning the female delinquent or her older counterpart, the female criminal. Most frequently this deletion was not even discussed. More rigorous researchers would, however, sometimes accompany their decision with sheepish apologies such as the following, which appeared as a footnote in Hirschi's *Causes of Delinquency*:

> In the analysis which follows, "non-Negro" becomes "white," and the *girls disappear* [emphasis added] . . . Since girls have been neglected for too long by students of delinquency, the exclusion of them is difficult to justify. I hope to return to them soon.[1]

When more thorough justifications for failing to include women in delinquency research were offered, they generally relied heavily on conventional stereotypes about male and female behavior. Albert Cohen, in his widely cited work, *Delinquent Boys*, provides one of the clearest examples of this approach. Because "boys collect stamps and girls collect boys," Cohen felt it followed that the "problems of adjustment of men and women, of boys and girls, arise out of quite different circumstances and press for quite different solutions." The delinquent, he concluded, was essentially "a rogue male."[2]

Criminologists' failure to address the issue of women and

crime has seriously hampered efforts to understand not only why, when, and how women deviate or commit delinquent offenses, but the equally important questions of why, when, and how the society responds to this behavior. Moreover, this pattern of neglect has permitted and encouraged general theory building and research that is profoundly flawed by monosexism.[3] It is not too much to say that any theory or theories of deviance failing to account for the behavior (either conforming or rule violating) of over half of the population cannot, in the final analysis, be considered sound.

In the last ten years, however, this pattern of scholarly neglect appeared to be reversed, as the female criminal and, to some extent, her younger counterpart, were suddenly propelled into the limelight. Unfortunately, while this attention was long overdue, it was less a product of intellectual thoroughness than it was an attempt to discover the much sought-after "dark side" of the women's liberation movement.[4]

There was literally a rush to study women and crime, as journalists, and some academics, began to capitalize on the popular idea that the women's movement was causing an increase in female delinquency and criminality. These writers were joined, shortly later, by many other academics who were drawn into the area simply because women had now become a fashionable topic of criminological research.

There has been, in short, a veritable explosion of writings on the female delinquent and her older counterpart, the female criminal. Regrettably, only some of this work can be said to have brought about a greater understanding of either the dynamics of female delinquency or the treatment of those young women who come into the criminal justice system. Many of these writings have, if anything, muddied the intellectual waters, and, in some instances, provided support for those who are seeking scientific legitimacy for patterns of personal and institutional sexism. To demonstrate this thesis, this paper will discuss two of the major anti-female themes in the emerging literature on female delinquency: the notion that the women's movement has caused younger women to seek equality in the area of crime; and the newer notion that, appearances to the contrary, the juvenile justice system does not actually discriminate against young women. In the course of reviewing the evidence on these two points, the more promising research trends in this area will also be explored.

When She's Bad She's Horrid

It was perhaps inevitable that women's attempts to secure equality and dignity for their sex would eventually result in the enthusiastic search for the negative consequences of such efforts. Historically, one of these has been the notion that granting women increased freedom would cause a corresponding growth in the amount of their criminal activity.[5] Moreover, there appeared to be some empirical evidence to support the idea that the most recent women's movement was, in fact, paralleling an increase in women's crime and particularly an increase in female delinquency.

Between 1960 and 1975 arrests of adult females were up 60.2 percent, while arrests of their younger counterparts increased by an alarming 253.9 percent. Along with these figures were even more dramatic increases in particular types of what might be called non-traditional female crime. Arrests of young women for forcible rape were up 466.7 percent, murder up 275 percent and robbery up a startling 647.8 percent.[6] Not surprisingly, first to make the connection between these changes in the number of women arrested and the then-burgeoning women's movement were law enforcement officials, many of whose agencies had been under substantial federal pressure to hire women. "The women's movement has triggered a crime wave like the world has never seen before," claimed Chief Ed Davis of the Los Angeles Police Department.[7] On another occasion, he expanded on his thesis by explaining that the "breakdown of motherhood" signalled by the women's movement could lead to "the use of dope, stealing, thieving and killing."[8] Other officials, such as Sheriff Pritchess of California, made less inflammatory comments that echoed the same general theme: "As women emerge from their traditional roles as housewife and mother, entering the political and business fields previously dominated by males, there is no reason to believe that women will not also approach equality with men in the criminal activity field."[9]

In the academic community, Freda Adler, in her book *Sisters in Crime*, also linked changes in the official arrest statistics to women's struggle for social and economic equality, thereby lending scientific credibility to the hypothesis.

> The movement for full equality has a darker side which has been slighted even by the scientific community . . . In the same way that women are demanding equal opportunity in the fields of legitimate endeavor, a similar number of determined women are forcing their way into the world of major crimes.[10]

While Adler's formulation met with wide public acceptance, more careful analysis of changes in women's arrest rates lends little support to this notion. Utilizing national arrest data supplied by the Federal Bureau of Investigation, along with more localized police and court statistics, Darrell Steffenmeier[11] examined the pattern of female criminal behavior for the years 1965-1977. After weighting the arrest data for changes in population, as well as comparing increases in female arrests to increases in male arrests, Steffensmeier concluded that "females are not catching up with males in the commission of violent, masculine, male-dominated serious crimes (except larceny) or in white collar crimes."[12] He did note female arrest gains in the Uniform Crime Report categories of larceny, fraud, forgery, and vagrancy but, by examining these gains more carefully, he demonstrated that they were due almost totally to increases in traditionally female criminal areas such as shoplifting, prostitution and naive check forgery (fraud).

Moreover, Steffenmeier noted that forces outside of women's behavior are probably responsible for changes in the numbers of adult women arrested in these traditionally female areas. The increased willingness of stores to prosecute shoplifters, combined with a declining use of this same arrest category to control public drunkenness; and the growing concern with "welfare fraud" are social factors which he suggested might explain changes in female arrests, without any necessary changes in the numbers of women involved in these activities.

Executing a similar analysis of the change in the official rates of juvenile female crime, Steffensmeier and Steffensmeier[13] came to much the same conclusion. They noted that most of the large increases in juvenile female arrests (between 1965 and 1977) occurred in the categories of larceny, liquor law violation, narcotic drug laws, and runaways. Moreover, in this same period, juvenile female arrest rates declined for gambling, curfew, sex offenses, vagrancy, and suspicion.[14] With regard to the areas of increase, the authors make two observations: first, like the offenses involved in the increase in adult female arrests, these juvenile offenses are "traditionally female"; and second, they are areas where changes in enforcement practices have occurred. There is no evidence in even the official statistics to conclude that young women were engaging in more "serious crime" in 1977 than were their counterparts in 1965. Almost all of the apparent support for that contention came from increases in the number of women arrested for shoplifting, underage drinking and marijuana use.[15]

The authors also reviewed data on court referrals for roughly the same period. They suggest that here, again, much of the increase observed in the number of females referred to court was due to increases in court referrals for shoplifting, marijuana, and drug use, and in status offenses such as running away or violating curfew. Finally, the authors note that many of these increases in both female arrest and referral rates have leveled off since 1970.

Another perspective on female deviant behavior comes from studies which solicit from young people, themselves, accounts of volume and frequency of illegal activity. A recent self-report study conducted by Weis[16] confirmed earlier findings that the volume of unreported female delinquency was substantial and also added another revealing aspect. Weis found the oft-cited 1:6 ratio of male to female arrestees to be twice as large as the mean ratio of 1:2.56 self-reported participants in actual delinquent behavior. More importantly, Weis was interested in exploring differences, over time, in the character and volume of self-reported delinquency to determine if, in fact, the women's movement had had any impact on the actual volume of female misbehavior. Comparing the findings of self-report studies conducted during 1960, 1964, 1968, and 1971, he showed that "the mean sex ratios across all delinquent acts and for theft and aggression items have not changed in the direction predicted by the 'liberation' theories for this time period."[17] He also noted that sex ratios across all offenses were "relatively stable" for the decade, contrary to the impression that they would become more narrow. Indeed, rates of violent behavior actually showed boys becoming more violent, while girls became less violent.

Gold, in his comparison of two national self-reported studies for the periods of 1967 and 1972, confirmed these general findings, with one important exception. Gold found that while girls in 1972 were reporting less larceny, property destruction, and breaking and entering, "they reported greater use of marijuana and alcohol which increased their overall amount of reported delinquency."[18] Steffensmeier and Steffensmeier, extending this analysis to three of the most recent self-report studies, concluded that male-female differences in self-reported delinquency had remained stable during the years 1972–1977, when, in their words, "the Women's Movement should have been having its greatest impact."[19] In short, though there may have been a slight increase in "deportment" offenses among young women, there is no support in these studies for the notion that dramatic changes in the type and level of female criminality have occurred as a "result" of the women's movement. If anything, these studies point to a leveling off of changes in both unofficial and official rates of female delinquent activity during the 1970's, which is precisely the period during which one would expect to see the greatest change, if the women's movement had, in fact, caused a change in the level of female deviance.

A different approach to the relationship between the women's movement and adolescent female criminality was utilized by James and Thornton.[20] Questioning 287 young women about their attitudes toward feminism and the extensiveness of their delinquent behavior, they found that attitudes toward feminism had little direct effect on social delinquency, but did have slight direct effects on property and aggressive delinquency. However, in the latter case, this influence was found to be *negative*—which clearly does not support the notion that the women's movement is providing attitudinal support for female entry into the criminal world. Indeed, this negative relationship held even when the young women were encountering such delinquency producing forces as "high degrees of delinquency opportunity," "social support for delinquency," and "low levels of parental control."[21]

Another set of self-report studies which confounded conventional wisdom in this area were those conducted by Norland, Wessel, and Shover, examining the relationship between masculine characteristics and delinquent behavior.[22] Again utilizing self-report data, the authors found that for males "masculinity" was directly related only to status offenses (i.e. not related to male participation in either property or aggressive offenses). For females, the authors found, surprisingly, that females with more masculine characteristics were "less involved" in delinquency than those reporting less masculine traits.

Finally, there is Rankin's research on the differences between male and female attitudes toward education and the relationship of these attitudes to delinquency.[23] Looking at both educational performance and attitudes toward the educational experience, Rankin expected to find that these factors would have a greater effect on male delinquent behavior than on female delinquency, since males have traditionally been seen as more directly affected by occupational achievement (or surrogates for this, such as educational success). He found that negative attitudes toward school and poor school performance were both significant in predicting delinquency but, contrary to his expectations, this relationship was stronger for girls than for boys.

Taken together, these studies indicate that there is little empirical support for the belief that the women's movement has inspired a crime wave among either young women or their older counterparts. More importantly, the studies undertaken to explore this relationship have revealed that many of the popular stereotypes about female and male delinquency must be discarded. Systematic research efforts exploring the relationship of masculine and feminine attributes to delinquent behavior need to continue. Additionally, the adequacy of theories of delinquent behavior that have been previously tested on all-male populations must be re-examined, and their assumptions re-researched. Some of this work is already underway, and as this review has shown, these studies are already providing information which will greatly advance the understanding of delinquency as a social phenomenon.[24]

This research is not solely of academic interest, however, as the absence of sound information about the causes of female delinquency has allowed stereotyped notions to contaminate those programs which have been designed to prevent it. Surveys of services to female delinquents consistently demonstrate that fewer programs are available to them, and that the programs which are provided for them are often sex stereotyped. For example, a study conducted by the Law Enforcement Assistance Administration revealed that between 1969 and 1975, only 5 percent of all federal juvenile justice funds were specifically designated for female-related programs. The local figures were not much better, with only 6 percent of the expenditures going for female programs.[25]

A look at the content of the programs offered for females makes the prospect for genuine assistance appear even dimmer. In a national survey of 107 state training schools, the American Bar Association found more female training schools than male had no training (15.8 percent compared to 4.7 percent).[26] Moreover, where training was taking place, the programs tended to prepare males for entry into relatively high paying positions (e.g., mechanic, carpenter, electrician), whereas most female training programs prepared young women for dead-end, low-paid, "women's work" (e.g., clerical work, housekeeping, cosmetology, waitressing, or nurse's-aide).[27]

A review of programs not confined to institutions yields much the same picture. Boisvert and Wells reviewed the treatment of male and female status offenders in the Worcester Family Court between 1973 and 1975 and found that courts were more likely to respond in a paternalistic manner to female than male status offenders. That is to say, they were far more willing to intervene in the lives of young women who came before them. For example, their data revealed that referrals for individual, group, or family counseling were made much more frequently for females (70.1 percent for the first offense) than for males (18.9 percent). Moreover, these referrals were not made in lieu of harsher sanctions, but in addition to them. Female first offenders were also far more likely than their male counterparts to be removed from their homes (i.e. placed in foster care, residential care, or detention services). In short, their offenses occasioned more official intervention because of what the authors described as "a sexist and paternalistic attitude in the human service delivery system."[28]

Clearly, too little is known and too much is assumed about the nature of female delinquency and possible strategies for its prevention. As the foregoing discussion has indicated, neither official records nor young women's self-reports bear out contentions of a dramatic increase in girls' illegal activities coincident with the rise of the women's movement. Furthermore, available evidence suggests that illegal behavior of girls has continued to be concentrated in the "female" areas of shoplifting, status offenses, and substance abuse. But in spite of the relatively unchanged volume and nature of youthful female crime, young women were arrested in increasing numbers during the 1970s, as were their older counterparts. Opponents of the women's movement seized this opportunity to lay blame upon female agitation for equality. Simultaneously, girl offenders provided a convenient scapegoat for those outraged by legitimate feminist political and social activity. This is as sad as it is ironic, inasmuch as female delinquents are among the most dependent, the poorest, and the most victimized (both physically and sexually) of all teenagers.[29] Yet the heaping of indignation upon these young women, largely victims, served to shift attention from their genuine and long-neglected needs at precisely the time when more and more of them were being drawn into the juvenile justice system.

Sexist Juvenile Justice: Fact or Artifact?

Female delinquents have not been the objects of serious scholarly research until very recently. Because of this pattern of neglect, not only was little known about the nature of female delinquency, but also the character of the official response to the youthful female offenders was never systematically examined.

In the absence of hard information about the actual experiences of young women who were brought into the juvenile justice system, a number of myths abounded. Probably the most significant of these were, first, the notion that young women, like their older counterparts, were treated "chivalrously," and, second, the assumption that when the court intervened in young women's lives, it was out of necessity. Implicit in the second assumption was the reassuring idea that programs for young women adequately met their needs and were, on the whole, beneficial and of less harsh consequence.

The chivalry hypothesis was largely an extension of a widely accepted assumption that, in the words of Otto Pollak, "men hate to accuse women and thus indirectly to send them to their punishment; police officers dislike to arrest them, district attorneys to prosecute them, judges and juries to find them guilty, and so on."[30] That this proposition has enjoyed wide acceptance is well documented,[31] as is the fact that it has been assumed that chivalry extended to girls:

> Finally, in crime a certain degree of chivalry prevails. Some people dislike to report a woman criminal to the police and the police are more likely to release women or turn a young woman over to her parents or release [her] to a social agency than would be true for boys or men.[32]

Another myth which co-existed with the chivalry hypothesis was the notion that treatment programs for women tended to be more benevolent and less harsh than those for males—that they afforded the delinquent female protection rather than punishment:

> The literature on the subject of delinquency in girls is not more than a small fraction of that relating to crime and delinquency in the male. This is so for many reasons. In the first place, the delinquent girl is much less frequent than her male counterpart; and in the second place she is criminologically much less interesting. Her offenses take predominately the form of sexual misbehavior; a kind to call for her care and protection rather than her punishment.[33]

Perhaps because female delinquents were criminologically "less interesting," the actual treatment they received in the juvenile justice system was rarely, if ever, explored. When the subject of female delinquency was discussed, it was often in a dismissive fashion that generally explained why the author did not plan to explore the topic. Moreover, the few who did write the most extensive discussions on the appropriate response to female delinquency were often, themselves, involved in the system, or were uncritical of the official response to female delinquents, or convinced of its justification:

> On first examination it would appear from these data that the court discriminates heavily against the female sex offender, even though the offense that brings her to the court is seldom, if ever, bizarre sex behavior characteristic of the male offender. Such an interpretation is, in our opinion, totally at variance with the

facts. Training schools are more frequently needed for the promiscuous female for her own protection.[34]

[The] sexually delinquent girl violates the caring and protective
attributes of her maternal role in a way which will harm her and
her offspring for the remainder of her life.[35]

While studying delinquent girls, we should keep this in mind:
when you train a man you train one individual; when you train a
woman, you train a family.[36]

Because of silence broken only by occasional rationalizations,
the actual character of the treatment of young women at the
hands of the juvenile justice system has remained obscure until
very recently, when feminist researchers began to explore the
anomalies in the existing literature on women labelled as delinquent.[37]

Feminists found problems with the conventional character-
izations of female delinquency, as well as with the received
opinion that young women were treated "chivalrously." With
reference to the nature of female delinquency, they found that
careful reading of self-reports of female and male delinquency
did not reflect reputed dramatic differences in misbehavior.
Indeed, it appeared that if juvenile courts were randomly sampl-
ing juvenile delinquents, court populations would contain fewer
females than males, but that both would be charged with roughly the same offenses.[38] Yet, an examination of public arrests and
official records of court populations show a preponderance of
young women are arrested and/or referred to court for "status
offenses" ("running away from home," being "incorrigible,"
"beyond control," truant, or a "person in need of supervision"), rather than for criminal offenses. Studies in Honolulu,[39]
New York,[40], Delaware,[41] New Jersey[42] and a large mid-western
city[43] show that roughly half of the young women referred to
court are status offenders. About a fifth to a quarter of the
males are referred for these offenses.

Laws against status offenses have long been criticized as
unconstitutionally vague and over-broad,[44] but more important
for the present discussion, such laws often provide buffer
charges for monitoring and punishing suspected female sexuality.[45]

Because these offense categories are essentially outgrowths of

the juvenile court's historic and uncritical endorsement of familial authority, they pose a unique threat to young women. The
family has always held two standards for evaluating misbehavior: one for sons and another for daughters. This traditional
"double standard" decrees that most youthful male misbehavior will be overlooked. Young men are actually encouraged to
challenge familial authority and to experiment sexually. Young
women, on the other hand, are socialized to be dependent and
obedient, and every incident of defiance is carefully scrutinized
for evidence of sexual activity.

The court's commitment to familial authority made it inevitable that these differential perceptions of male and female delinquency would be built into the juvenile justice system's functioning. Images of the "fallen woman" and excessive concern
with sexual matters haunted the earliest writings on female
delinquency. Historians Steven Scholossman and Stephanie
Wallach document, for example, the first family court's charac-
terization of female delinquency "wholly in sexual terms" as
well as the court's harsh and Victorian response to this behavior.[46]

Nor is this pattern restricted to past history. The language of
status offense laws invites, according to one student of the
court, "discretionary" application of their provisions and
"allows parents, police, and juvenile court authorities, who
ordinarily decide whether PINS proceedings should be initiated,
to hold girls legally accountable for behavior—often sexual or in
some way related to sex—that they would not consider serious
if committed by boys."[47]

Essentially, all youthful female misbehavior is subject to surveillance for evidence of sexual misconduct. The process of
sexualization of female deviance is highly significant, as a study
by Smith demonstrates. Interviewing young women in a British
family court (most were referred for status offenses), Smith discovered that many reported very high rates of typically male
criminal acts such as "deliberate property damage" (68 percent), gang fighting (63 percent), joy riding (60 percent) and
breaking and entering (33 percent). To explain partly why the
young women were not charged with these offenses, Smith cites
interviews that indicated that "non-sexual offenses were overlooked in favor of sexual misbehavior" by court officials:

It's funny because once when I was down the cop shop for fighting, this woman saw the swastika on my arm and forgot all
about what she was looking for. They never did nothing—just
told me to stop fighting. But the woman cop, she kept on about
the swastika and Hell's Angels. What a bad lot they were for a
girl to go around with and how I had better stop going around
with the Angels or else I'd get a really bad name for myself. Then
she kept asking me if I'd had sex with any of 'em or taken
drugs.[48]

Earlier research indicated the existence of this pattern.[49] All
females admitted to Honolulu's family court during the 1950s,
for example, were given physical examinations to determine
whether they had had sexual contact, and the findings of these
exams were often added to the charges against the young
women. Indeed physical examinations of young women for evidence of venereal disease, pregnancy, or substance use are routine in many jurisdictions, regardless of the nature of the charge
brought against the young woman.[50] It is clear that these
examinations are not only degrading but also serve to remind all
woman that any form of deviance will be defined as evidence of
sexual laxity. Consistent with this, young women arrested or
referred for status offenses are not treated chivalrously. Instead,
at every level of court processing, young women charged with
these offenses are harshly punished.

One of the most thorough investigations of this phenomenon,
by Datesman and Scarpatti,[51] examined court dispositions of
referrals for one Delaware family court. By controlling for
offense, they found that at every stage of judicial decision-
making (from intake to institutionalization), female status
offenders received the harshest sanctions. For example, 8 percent of the females whose first offense was a status offense were
institutionalized, compared to only 2 percent of the males
charged with felonies, less than 1 percent of the males charged
with misdemeanors and 5 percent of the males charged with
status offenses. For repeat status offenses, females were six
times more likely than their male counterparts to be institutionalized.[52]

Predictably, there are now several pieces of research which
dispute the findings that reveal a clear picture of institutional
sexism within the juvenile court. Almost without exception,

these studies employ statistical techniques which attempt to "control" for the effects of other variables known to affect judicial outcomes (prior record, type of offense, income, ethnicity, relationship with family, etc.), and then explore the residual differences in the treatment of males and females by judicial agencies. On the surface, such a methodology appears sound, but a closer look at two recent studies shows clear difficulties with such an approach.

Teilmann and Landry,[53] for example, examined police and court dispositions of youthful offenders in several locations for evidence of "gender bias." These authors relied heavily on data drawn from a five-state study of services to status offenders, though they also used some California data on police dispositions of both criminal and status offenders. By controlling for "offense type" and "prior record," the authors found that "status offenders are consistently given harsher treatment than delinquent offenders" but, they continued, "this is true for boys as it is for girls." From this, they concluded that treatment within the court was "relatively even-handed."[54]

In the case of the Teilmann and Landry research, only two such "controls" were employed, while in other studies even more detail was employed. For example, a study of two North Carolina courts by Clarke and Koch[55] (who also concluded that gender had "little or no effect" on official treatment) segregated out the effects of many extra-legal factors, as well as variables directly related to the criminal history of the minor. Included in these were such factors as "the child's family structure," "support of lack thereof by the family as shown by court attendance," and whether the complainant in the case was a parent or a police officer. They also controlled for the effects of being held in detention. In this research, the authors concluded that while gender had "no effect," they were surprised to discover that youth brought to court by their parents and charged with non-criminal status offenses stood greater likelihood of adjudication and commitment than did their counterparts charged with felonies.[56]

Essentially, these studies have statistically segregated those elements in the juvenile justice system which make women uniquely vulnerable to harsh sanctions, and have then concluded that there is no evidence of bias against women. For example it is known that males commit as many status offenses as females, and yet women are over-represented among those charged with offenses. Even in their report, Teilmann and Landry present data on this point. Comparing girls' contributions to arrests for runaway and incorrigible with girls' self-reports of these two activities, they found a 10.4 percent over-representation of females among those arrested for runaway and 30.9 percent over-representation in arrests for incorrigibility. From this, they concluded that girls "are arrested for status offenses at a higher rate than boys, when contrasted to their self-reported delinquency rates."[57]

Both of these studies also noted, one directly from their data and one indirectly, that estrangement from parents negatively affected official response to the youth brought into the system. Yet, it is known that young women are more likely to be referred by their parents than are their male counterparts. Rosemary Sarri has estimated that about one third of all girls, but only one tenth of all boys, are referred to court by their parents.[58] This disparity is likely a product of parental bias in the assessment of the seriousness of male and female misconduct.

Finally, Clarke and Kock noted that "being held in detention before the court hearing made commitment more likely."[59] Again, it is known that young women charged with status offenses are more likely to be detained while awaiting court hearings. Indeed, even Teilmann and Landry found clear evidence in the five sites they studied that a larger percentage of females than males were detained. In one of these sites (northern California), that difference reached 22.3 percent. Moreover, by looking at detention rates for two major types of status offenses (incorrigible and runaway) for each site (or 10 possible figures), the data show that in eight of these, the proportion of girls who were detained exceeded that of the boys (though in some cases the differences were small in magnitude). Yet, curiously, the authors conclude from these data that "there is no real pattern across sites on detention variables."[60] Finally, the actual number of young women charged with status offenses (and detained) exceeded the males in every site.

Two other studies[61] also found evidence which appears, superficially, to support the conclusion that male and female status offenders are equally penalized. Andrews and Cohn examined the processing of status offenders in the New York State Family Courts. They found, when comparing females and males brought in to a probation officer as "PINS" (Person In Need of Supervision), that males were slightly more likely to be referred to court (65 percent versus 57 percent) and, once in the court, slightly more likely to be adjudicated (53 percent compared to 43 percent). However, they also noted that "when allegations of sexual activity are present, cases are sent to court at a rate higher than the norm." These cases, they observe elsewhere in a footnote, were almost always females.

More importantly, a closer look at the content of these PINS petitions revealed that a substantial number of youth in this category were alleged to have committed criminal violations. Andrews and Cohn noted here that "while substantial numbers of both boys and girls are involved [in this group], the boys tend to be primarily in court for physical violence or crimes against property or persons of others, while girls are primarily accused of abusing drugs or alcohol.[62] The appearance of criminal allegations on status offender petitions is, itself, a significant finding, and it assuredly indicates that general data on court dispositions of these "status offense" cases will be somewhat difficult to interpret.

Lawrence Cohen, in his study of delinquency dispositions in three juvenile courts, found that, after controlling for prior arrests, age, race, formality of the complaint, socio-economic status, family stability, and detention status, there was little difference in severity of disposition by sex. Again, however, it is clear that controlling for "family stability" and "detention status" will certainly wash out important differences in the treatment of female and male delinquents.

Indeed, Lawrence Cohen and James Kluegal, in two more recent papers[63] looked at these same data more closely and came to some slightly revised conclusions. Most notably, they found that sex of the offender did affect decision-making at both the level of intake and detention, with young women accused of "decorum" offenses (alcohol and drug referrals) penalized. Also, in one of the two courts studied, female status offenders, in general, were more likely to be detained than their male counterparts. Cohen and Kluegal suggested that the likely explanation for these differences was the fact that "both courts operate on a double standard of behavior,'' reacting ''more negatively toward females for moral reasons more often than males, and males for criminal reasons more often than females.''[64]

In most of these studies there is a background assumption that behaviors which constitute a male status offense are essentially equivalent to those which constitute female status offenses. However, detailed research on this point by Boisvert and Wells found ''a significant difference'' in the types of status complaints brought against males and females in Massachusetts.[65] Males, the researchers found, were more likely to be defined as ''stubborn children,'' while females were more likely to be cast as ''runaways.'' Moreover, these researchers confirmed Andrews and Cohn's finding that male status offenders were more likely than females to have engaged in criminal misconduct. This study also refuted findings that female and male status offenders were likely to be equitably treated. They found that girls were far more likely than boys to be removed from their homes on a first referral to court for a status offense: 46.3 percent compared to 17.2 percent (though this pattern appeared to erode with subsequent referrals).

In total, a very close look must be taken at the technique of ''controlling'' for the effects of variables which are themselves elements of the pattern of institutional sexism which victimizes women. To gain a fuller understanding of the workings of these patterns of institutional sexism (or racism, for that matter), there must be a shift away from passive data collection (e.g., analysis of court statistics) to a closer examination of the organizational processes which both generate these data and, more importantly, handle youth.

One model for this research is Albert J. Reiss' review of 1,500 cases of alleged sexual misbehavior heard by one metropolitan juvenile court judge. He noted that this judge:

> . . . refused to treat any form of sexual behavior on the part of boys, even the most bizarre forms, as warranting more than probationary status. The judge, however, regarded girls as the ''cause'' of sexual deviation in boys in all cases of coition involving an adolescent couple and refused to hear the complaints of the girl and her family; the girl was regarded as a prostitute.[66]

A more recent investigation also underscores the necessity of examining court records carefully. Linda Hancock examined the actual content of police referrals of males and females to family courts in Australia and found that the sexual and moral activities of females were cited in 40 percent of the reports which referred the girls to court, but in only 5 percent of the reports on the male cases. Moreover, explicit mention of sexual intercourse was made in 29 percent of the reports referring females to court but in only 1 percent of the male cases. Hancock concluded that "this finding illustrates very clearly the sexualization of female delinquency and the relative lack of attention to sexual 'misbehavior' on the part of boys."[67] Her findings also provide an important context for Andrews and Cohn's footnote regarding the harsh official response to sexual misbehavior in New York.

What is needed to assess the meaning of official data are studies such as Hancock's which probe beneath the surface of the numbers. Moreover, though more time-consuming, direct observation in police cars, in probation offices, and in courtrooms is necessary before the meaning of the numerical or official data can emerge.

The meaning of contemporary data can also be more accurately assessed if placed in historical context. Here a good model exists in the fine work of Schlossman and Wallach in their study of the Chicago and Milwaukee courts.[68] This research documented both the fact that young women in the early years of these courts were prosecuted almost exclusively for "immoral conduct" (which was a category that "defined all sexual exploration as fundamentally perverse") and the fact that the court sent enormous numbers of women to reformatories for such behavior. For example, they noted that in Chicago between 1899 and 1909, one-half of the young women, but only one-fifth of the young men who came before that city's juvenile court were institutionalized.

Another valuable study is Sheldon's content analysis of the Memphis Family Court records in the early 1900s. This research also confirms the importance of the sexualization of female delinquency. Noting that while many young women were brought into the court for "dependency" or offenses other than "immorality," the author observed that the social files often indicated that these charges had "sexual overtones." Thus, in

Sheldon's words, in "about one third of all female cases" immorality was either the actual charge or the implied reason behind the charge."[69] Sheldon also noted that when sexual misconduct was suspected, a vaginal examination was given to determine whether or not the young woman had had intercourse.

Finally, more research must also be conducted on the impact of such recent developments as federal efforts to "de-institutionalize" status offenders, begun in 1974. How have young women who find their way into the court been affected by de-institutionalization efforts? Tony Hoffman's preliminary work on practices in Oregon gives some information on this point.[70] Hoffman noted that there was a "significant" drop in the total commitments of young women to training schools in Oregon between the years 1973 and 1980 as a result of juvenile code changes intended to prevent the incarceration of status offenders. However, Hoffman was quick to point out that this did not signal equity for young women in the juvenile justice system in Oregon.

Hoffman found, for example, little evidence that things had improved much for young female status offenders at the level of detention, noting that 16.9 percent of the females charged with status offenses but only 11.2 percent of females charged with crimes, were detained. In contrast, 55.7 percent of males charged with crimes and 16.2 percent of males charged with status offenses were detained. In essence, male and female status offenders seem equally likely to be detained in Oregon, but the female status offender is more likely to be detained than her criminal counterpart, while the reverse is true for males.

At the level of commitment to training schools, Hoffman found another intriguing pattern. Nearly half (43 percent) of the females committed to Oregon's training schools between 1977–1980, but only 16 percent of the males, were incarcerated for misdemeanors. In contrast, over a third of the males (34.1 percent) but only about a tenth (11.8 percent) of the females were incarcerated for Class A felonies. In short, while incarcerations of young women are declining, women still appear to be incarcerated for far less serious offenses than their male counterparts.

In general, however, it does appear that some of the de-institutionalization efforts have served to limit the court's discretion and, as a consequence, fewer young women are being institutionalized. National figures show, for example, that between 1973 and 1977, the number of young women held in short-term facilities dropped by 36.3 percent, and the number of young women held in long term facilities dropped by nearly the same percentage (30.5 percent). Between 1977 and 1979, this decline continued, with female commitments to short term facilities dropping another 10 percent and their commitments to long term facilities declining by 19 percent.[71] Figures on the number of males and females in private juvenile facilities showed a similar decline; between 1974 and 1979 the number of females held in both short term and long term custody facilities dropped by 15.3 percent, while the male figure dropped by only 7.2 percent.[72]

Federal cutbacks, however, particularly those which jeopardize alternative programs and shelter care for status offenders bode ill for young women. The prospects for reform grow still more dim as federal cutbacks coincide with the rise of a vigorous right wing movement. Among other prime objectives, this movement seeks to empower the traditional family's control over young people.[73] These forces are joined by those who are, in their exaggerated fear of juvenile crime, urging the criminal justice system to adopt a harsh and punitive response to virtually all youthful misbehavior.[74]

Conclusions

All of these cross-currents need to be taken into account as research proceeds on the court's treatment of young women. What is abundantly clear is that young women's deviance and the official response to that behavior have, until recently, not been the objects of serious research. Interest has now been awakened, but it is unclear whether this new attention will bring benefit to young women. As has been shown, numerous efforts have been made to link a "rise in female crime" to the women's movement; more recently, studies which purport to explore the question of discrimination against women in the juvenile system have used techniques which serve to obfuscate institutional sexism within that system. These trends are, to some extent, balanced by the more promising research which has also been briefly discussed here. These latter studies are stripping away the myths surrounding both the character of female misbehavior and the typical responses to that behavior.

While it is encouraging that some progressive research is underway, much more work remains to be done, particularly work focussing on official responses to young women's deviance. Unfortunately, it is always easier to study the youthful female offender than to study those who label and treat her. She is virtually powerless, while those who process her are not. If, however, researchers succumb to the temptation of examining the young female offender, but neglect the study of official agencies of social control, they run the serious risk of never developing a full understanding of female delinquency. But perhaps even more importantly, an institution with a very bad track record of according women fair treatment will be allowed to function with virtually no oversight.

In sum, then, all aspects of female delinquency must be explored. The past scholarly indifference and silence allowed a great injustice to be ignored. The new interest in the young female offender must be informed by awareness of the complexities of her condition, as well as respectful of young women themselves, in order that their oppression will never again be relegated to a footnote.

Easy Money
Adolescent Involvement in Prostitution

Debra Boyer
Jennifer James

Introduction

The young woman involved in prostitution has made a sex role choice which clearly carries a negative label: that of the whore.[1] Why do some young women make this choice, while others do not? Traditional theories of female deviance have not adequately explained the process of entrance into juvenile prostitution for several reasons. These theories accept the "normal" roles assigned to women and men in society, and primarily, the restrictions placed upon female sexual behavior as compared to that of males. In the case of prostitution, female sexuality has been criminalized, for while the male client's behavior may be regarded as normal, that of the prostitute is not. Further, the illicit sexuality of the male poses no threat to established institutions. Women have been disproportionately punished for prostitution because society views the open sexuality of the female prostitute as a threat to family structure.

The young woman contemplating entrance into prostitution, like any other young woman, has been conditioned to societal expectations of female and male sexual behavior. The choice to prostitute, therefore, reflects acceptance of a deviant self-concept. Traditional studies have neglected or misinterpreted the factors contributing to the delinquent female's internalization of a deviant identity.

Literature Review

The literature on juvenile criminal activity has provided only limited information on juvenile prostitution. Studies on adult prostitutes have provided a retrospective view of the motivations for entrance by juveniles. The motivations for entrance into prostitution, according to studies of adult prostitutes, can be divided into three categories: 1) conscious; 2) situational; 3) psychoanalytical.

Conscious Motivations

Economic circumstances are cited repeatedly in the literature. Prostitution is seen as an occupational choice affording the highest attainable standard of living for low-skilled or unskilled women.[2] It is sometimes observed that the influence or coercion of a man/pimp is an immediate cause of entrance into prostitution.[3] Certain writers point out that prostitution offers alternative working conditions to "routine and confining jobs" of traditional female employment.[4] Finally, the fast life of prostitution according to some writers, is attractive because it offers adventure, glamour, and an opportunity to meet interesting people.[5]

Situational Motivations

Parental abuse, physical abuse, neglect, and generally poor relationships with parents are commonly reported for women involved in prostitution.[6] Early life experiences, particularly early sexual experience and traumatic events such as rape and incest, are cited as important in entrance into prostitution.[7] Exposure and access to prostitution during childhood through relatives or through the neighborhood environment may be a significant factor in entrance into prostitution for some women, according to some researchers.[8] Additionally, it has been observed that low status service occupations lead women into prostitution.[9]

Psychoanalytical Motivations

Homosexuality has been viewed as a neurotic component of prostitution motivation.[10] It has been suggested that homosexuality represents an inability to develop normal sexual identity, with prostitution representing an attempt to deny homosexual inclinations.[11] Prostitution has also been seen as an atonement for guilt produced by incestuous fantasies;[12] as a manifestation of frigidity;[13] as motivated by hostility towards men; and as a striving for reassurance of physical attractiveness.[14]

Juvenile Prostitution

Theories about juvenile involvement in prostitution rely primarily on studies of adults, such as those cited above. The general literature on female delinquents seldom explicitly mentions prostitution, but discussions of female delinquency and female sexuality are generally linked together. The result is that a number of studies identify the female delinquent as promiscuous; i.e., as a sexual delinquent.[15] The literature on actual prostitution, however, is both limited and ambivalent.

Literature on juveniles often reflects disbelief that young women involve themselves in prostitution.[16] These findings are at odds with the statistical increase in juvenile prostitution.[17] There are few empirical studies that have concentrated on prostitution. Gray's study of twenty juvenile prostitutes focused on the pre-existing conditions necessary to make a girl vulnerable to prostitution.[18] Her findings support causation in tense family relationships, broken homes, and low social-economic status, which lead the young women to seek out positive reinforcement in nonconventional ways.

More general literature on the sexual nature of female delinquency points out that prostitution may often be an activity hidden formally, but acknowledged informally. It is generally accepted that a status offense is often a euphemism for a sexual offense committed by juvenile females.[19] The assumed sexual nature of young women's offenses has led to three basic theories of female juvenile delinquency.[20] Psychoanalysts find the roots of delinquency in disturbed family relationships.[21] The broken home is a major factor in the findings of several writers, who also place considerable emphasis on chromosomal and physiological factors, such as "bigness."[22] Loneliness, dependency, and non-fulfillment of the female sex role are also seen as causal.[23] Socially negative reactions to any deviance from the female sex role is suggested as a precipitant to delinquency by various writers.[24] The sexuality of juvenile women as the root of delinquency is discussed most often in terms of promiscuity. Promiscuity is often traced to oedipal family relationships.[25]

Promiscuity is also ascribed to "female" emotions of dependency and loneliness.[26] Other environmental causes—social, economic, changing values—have not been investigated adequately. Demographic characteristics on female juveniles, with some exceptions, are seldom gathered methodically, leaving conclusions to be drawn from case studies.[27]

Entrance into prostitution by juveniles has been studied in some detail by Gray and by Kagan.[28] The first, as noted previously, concentrated on a small sample (20) utilizing only a limited interview format. The second study concentrated on a theoretical evaluation of symbolic and non-symbolic behavior in both sexual promiscuity and prostitution among juvenile females. Both behaviors are seen as a reflection of social and cultural forces operating in contemporary society; e.g., disintegration of the family, impersonal communities, and conflicting norms and values.

Most of the studies cited here represent traditional theories of female deviance. They do not describe the process of entrance into prostitution. The motivations towards prostitution listed here could be found in any random group of women. In addition, many of these theories have now been challenged by a number of researchers because of their "conceptual neglect of the sex variable,"[29] and because of their sexist definitions of deviance.[30] The traditional explanations for female deviance and motivations for prostitution have failed to identify the relationship of prostitution to female sexuality and the female gender role.

Several researchers have recently examined prostitution from the woman's point of view. These studies take into consideration the force of cultural stereotypes which classify females as "good women" (madonnas) or "bad women" (whores) on the basis of their conformity to societal norms or expectations. Traditionally, women have been expected to function in the sexual, biological, and service roles of wife and mother, exchanging the exercise of those functions for economic support. The prostitute functions within the traditional pattern, with the important difference that the barter aspect is open, and that the prostitute is not the exclusive sexual property of an individual male; hence, she cannot be a "good woman." Rosenblum argues that "prostitution utilizes the same attributes characteristic of the female sex role, and uses those attributes to the same ends; . . . the transition from non-deviance to deviance within prostitution requires only an exaggeration of the situation experienced as a non-deviant woman."[31] The degree to which a woman's sexual behavior falls into accepted patterns will determine whether she is perceived and labeled as good or bad, fixing her position in the madonna/whore spectrum. Sexual activity or promiscuity may precipitate a "drift" into prostitution based on "the internalization of a deviant self-concept in response to informal labeling, public branding, and subsequent stimatization," according to N. Davis.[32] James and Vitaliano have associated the development of a deviant sexual self-image in adolescence with a sexually deviant lifestyle as an adult.[33] More specifically, the relationship between early sexual experiences and prostitution has been argued by James and Meyerding.[34]

In this paper, we will examine juvenile prostitution in the context of the cultural roles assigned to females, with particular attention to the significance of early sexual experience in the forming of a deviant self-image. Our discussion is based in part on information gathered in ethnographic field work among juvenile prostitutes, as well as interviews of 138 adolescent female prostitutes and a control sample of 100 non-sexually labeled female delinquents.[35]

Juvenile Prostitutes

Adolescent involvement in prostitution has increased at an alarming rate. Between 1969 and 1978 there was a 183.3 percent increase in female juvenile prostitution and a 244.9 percent increase in male prostitution.[36] Total arrests do not represent the actual numbers of juvenile prostitutes. It is estimated that there are 600,000 female and 300,000 male juvenile prostitutes in the United States.[37] Some are as young as eight years old; most are between twelve and sixteen. The majority of adolescent prostitutes are initially runaways or abandoned children. Police estimate that as many as 1,000,000 children run away every year. Once separated from their families, few have access to legitimate means of support.

Prostitution is one of the most self-destructive activities in which a young person can engage. The isolation and risks of the "fast life" hold great danger of permanent psychological and physical damage. Adolescent prostitutes also fail to acquire the educational and occupational skills they will need in order to succeed legitimately as adults. We are just beginning to understand the effects of disrupted psycho-sexual development in juvenile prostitutes, nor have we developed solutions to the immediate problems they present. Social workers for example, are well aware of the difficulties of offering alternatives to the "fast life" of prostitution, and of disheartening failures.

Young women who see prostitution as an acceptable option can be loosely classified as: 1) deprived or disadvantaged; 2) physically and/or sexually abused; and 3) affluent and over-indulged. Females involved in prostitution are, of course, not one-dimensional. Their individual histories are complicated, especially in terms of the development of their sexuality. It is important to understand this development in the context of their immediate situations, which constrain the choices they perceive as available to them.

Deprived

Adolescent prostitutes who are deprived and disadvantaged are generally from low socio-economic status families and ethnic groups with a history of discrimination. These young women have either been denied or inconsistently provided with the physical necessities of life. Prostitution is an obvious way to avoid a life of poverty. Access to prostitution is usually available in the neighborhood or through a relative who is involved in prostitution. A mother, sister, or aunt involved in prostitution provides a model, and often facilitates entrance into the profession. These adolescents may also be prestigmatized, losing status because of community knowledge of a relative who is a known prostitute, even without engaging in prostitution themselves. Labeling by association, combined with economic factors, increases the motivation to prostitute.

Economics is an important precipitator of prostitution for women from all social classes and ethnic backgrounds. If you are at an economic disadvantage, prostitution can provide a source of income for insuring survival and achieving a sense of power and control over your life. James has argued that prostitution is a valid occupational choice for all low-skilled or un-skilled women who have been routinely denied access to legiti-mate educational and occupational opportunities and who must be self-supporting.[38] If men who can provide support are inac-cessible, or if the male supporter leaves, prostitution can be-come the only alternative to poverty. Prostitution is realistic and reasonable to the adolescent woman who is poor, lacks models of females who are successful in legitimate occupations, has little encouragement or opportunity to realize more acceptable aspirations, and whose imagination presents only the continua-tion of defeating experiences.

Abused

The physical and sexual abuse of children is not restricted by boundaries of class, ethnicity, or gender. Reports of victims and offenders come from all levels of our society. It is difficult to know actual numbers, but reports of social workers and system-atic studies indicate that between 40 and 75 percent of adoles-cent prostitutes, both male and female, are the victims of prior physical abuse, sexual abuse, or both. In a study by James (1977–1980) of 138 juvenile prostitutes, 37 percent had been molested, 51 percent raped and 63 percent reported physical abuse.[39] In an earlier study (1970–1971) of twenty adolescent female prostitutes, 65 percent (13) had been the victims of coerc-ed sexual activities.[40] In a sample of 136 adult prostitutes inter-viewed between 1974–75, 57 percent had been raped; 12 percent had experienced sexual advances by fathers prior to their own initiation into sexual activity.[41] The effect on child victims of sexual assault is significant. The imposition of adult sexuality on children disrupts psycho-sexual development. In the cases of very young children, it can retard physical development as well. A number of researchers have noted the effects on behavior of incest victims including promiscuity,[42] disruptive and rebellious behavior,[43] reactions of guilt, shame, and loss of self-esteem.[44]

Children are disturbed by sexual approaches; their inexperi-ence makes them both fearful and curious. Incest victims, for example, often blame themselves. They are caught in a conflict of divided loyalties within the family. They do not feel that they can tell the truth, and must live with feelings of guilt, terror, and confusion. Molested children feel helpless to change their situation, yet still culpable because they have done nothing about it. Once identified, the victim of incest faces serious disruption of a family which may already be deviant and highly disorganized. The victim suffers both as an abused individual and as a family member. The behavior of the victim and reactions to that behavior become significantly disorganizing factors in his or her development of sexual identity.[45]

The disruptive effect of sexual abuse is often manifested in adolescent behavior. At puberty, victims of sexual abuse often realize that their experiences are much different from those of their friends; and they begin to withdraw socially. Their guilt and confusion pervades other relationships. The normal developmental pathways of childhood are obstructed by sexual abuse, preventing the individualization crucial to adolescence. For example, there are indications that these adolescents hold a distorted image of their own bodies as the result of violation of their physical boundaries. Such violations may also lead them to expect that their worth will only be acknowledged when they permit sexual access.

Early, traumatic sexual self-objectification may be one factor which influences some women to enter into prostitution. Sexual self-objectification is experienced by all women in this society to some degree, because of the simultaneous cultural adoration and vilification of the female body and its sexuality (the madonna/whore spectrum). The guilt, shame, and loss of self-esteem resulting from being used sexually at an early age increase the likelihood of the victim's viewing herself as a salable commodity.[46]

Our society still functions with a double standard of sexual behavior for men and women. Women who engage in sexual activity outside of marriage, including sexual victims, are often stigmatized and lose status. They cannot fulfill the "good girl" image because of their sexual experience. Women who have been sexually abused often accept the label of "bad woman."

Physical and sexual abuse lessen the female victim's sense of self-worth and sexual self-respect. Our informal interviews with adolescent male prostitutes indicate a similar reaction. We suspect that a prior history of abuse may be found equally in male and female prostitutes. A feeling of lost manhood and abuse of the masculine image may play a large role in male entrance into prostitution.

The healthy choice for victims of physical and sexual abuse is to get out of the abusive situation. Our society, however, is lacking in sympathy and resources for the abused adolescent. Alternative economic and emotional support systems do not exist for the adolescent who cannot go home. Prostitution offers the economic means necessary to remain independent of an abusive home situation. Street companions provide friendship and understanding which were missing in homes or legal placements.

Affluent

Adolescents classified as affluent and over-indulged are not immune to either physical and sexual abuse or various forms of neglect. Traumatic and hurtful events are commonly found complicating individual lives. But traumatic events alone are not sufficient to lead young people to prostitution. We can distinguish unique influences leading the affluent to prostitution that are distinctive from those who are deprived or abused.

The rise of prostitution among the affluent is peculiarly associated with the socio-political values of the 1970's and 1980's. It may explain the increase in juvenile prostitution, or at least the recent attention and concern. The affluent adolescent prostitute has succumbed to strong social pressures to be sexually accomplished; she measures self-worth both in terms of seductive prowess and money-making ability. Still other conditions of an affluent lifestyle may make prostitution alluring. Middle- and upper-class girls admit to being very bored, to being spoiled, and to feeling resistance to over-protection. They may feel that they lead temperate lives, undefined by extremes of either joy or pain. They may be trained to passivity, expecting to be provided with entertainment and amusement.

Dependent upon tenuous vogue as a substitute for individuality, the affluent adolescent often has a sense that she is non-descript. Dressing up and visiting the streets with friends may offer a means of self-definition as well as diversion. It is exciting and satisfying to con, to cajole, to be aggressive. The extravagant sensations which may be derived from the illegality, immorality, and danger of prostitution are a relief from the neutrality of affluent life. Some young women have compared prostitution to shoplifting a generation ago. It is simply something new to be tried, the satisfaction of a curiosity for experience. For some, prostituting is like trying the first joint of marijuana; it is "another high."

The lifestyle of prostitution appears glamorous to many juveniles. The lifestyle is easy to imitate, and attention is an immediate reward. The clothes, the fast money, the games, and the men who are attracted provide the young female with an identity and an assurance that she has become a woman. Prostitution and life on the street are a testing ground for an adolescent's capabilities. Affluent adolescents seem to hunger for the confidence that they could survive the loss of affluence.

Affluence does not assure that children will suffer no neglect. Parents who are good material providers may have insufficient time or energy for adequate personal involvement with their children. Caretaker or custodial parenting sometimes causes children to feel angry, depressed, and lonely, anxious to experiment with anything that may fill the void. Affluent conditions may combine encouragement of experience for its own sake with a high degree of permissiveness. While the latter may be benign, it can also be a form of neglect, as adolescents, faced with decisions that may have harmful consequences, do not get help in making those decisions. Such a vacuum is especially likely to exist in the matter of adolescent decisions concerning sexuality. Few parents are able to acknowledge the sexuality of their children. Fewer still are able to discuss values and offer guidelines regarding sexual activity for young people.

Adolescent sexual behavior is heavily influenced by the varied private and situational circumstances just discussed. Additionally, juveniles cannot escape historical and cultural forces that affect their social development. These forces pervade the lives of children and have an impact on adolescent entrance into prostitution.

Status of Children

The history of children has been one filled with abuse. Children have been subjected to forced labor in unhealthy environments with minimum compensation. Historically, they have not been protected against abuse or granted personal rights. In law, children have been regarded as the personal property of their parents and treated as such. In spite of a slowly growing movement on behalf of children, information gathered in 1979, the International Year of the Child, suggests that conditions remain unimproved for millions of children. Although in our country child labor legislation has existed for many years and public welfare systems have been created, the legal rights and social status of minors are still quite limited.

In the largely rural societies of past centuries, children were an economic necessity; now children are an economic liability. At the same time that childbearing has to a large degree become a matter of choice, the purpose of having children has become unclear. For many, the long-term investment required for rearing children is incongruous with the demands and conditions of contemporary life. There is little prestige in having children, and very limited social support for child care and child rearing.

The mother who stays at home to rear her children finds only the most minimal reward and status in our society. Others who care for children are similarly unrewarded. Daycare workers are among the lowest-paid personnel in this country. Institutional staff responsible for problem, delinquent, and disturbed children are often untrained, unskilled, and underpaid. Dwindling financial support of schools in many areas is further evidence of our society's low regard for the importance of children. In short, there is small respect or praise for those entrusted with the care and guidance of the next generation.

Adolescents in particular are regarded largely as a burdensome charge. Many young people themselves perceive this social reality. Our lack of genuine concern for children is reflected in the 1,000,000 who run away each year, the 2,000,000 who are battered in their homes, the 1 in 10 adolescent girls who become pregnant,[47] the 1 in 5 who are sexually abused before they are eighteen,[48] and the thousands who survive economically and personally through prostitution.

Adolescents

The promotion of sexuality through every popular medium in society in recent decades has had a significant impact on the incidence of juvenile prostitution. Adolescents today are under intense pressure to be sexually attractive and sexually experienced. In spite of the earlier average age at which menarche and secondary sexual development are occurring now, few girls in their early teens are physically and emotionally prepared for sexual experience. The remarks of adolescent prostitutes about their initial sexual experiences express the ambivalence felt by young females themselves.

"I did it to get it over with."

"I have to be high to have sex."

"Sex doesn't do anything for me."

"Boy called me a slut anyway, so I finally did it."

Our society has been caught unprepared for the growing number of adolescents experiencing sex at an ever younger age. While adolescents occasionally receive technical information, questions of sexual values are largely avoided by their mentors. The result is confusion and distortion. For example, most sexually active adolescents do not realize that they can say no to sexual activity, nor are they taught to assert and defend themselves against exploitative situations. The increased sexual activity of adolescents, without the benefit of information and guidance, results in high teenage pregnancy and venereal disease rates. Our unwillingness to face the needs of adolescents also makes them vulnerable to sexual abuse and exploitation, particularly in the form of juvenile prostitution.

It is also necessary to recognize the economic situation of adolescents living in a society oriented to consumption, in which the pressures to consume are reinforced with every new and passing commercial fashion. Adolescents are especially sensitive to peer acceptance and vulnerable to peer influence. Nothing seems worse to teenagers than to be considered odd or to be ostracized because they are unable to do what their peers are doing and own what their peers own. Yet concerts, records, movies, cars, gasoline, and clothes are very expensive. At a time when experienced professional adults are unable to find employment, it is obvious that inexperienced and unskilled juveniles are unlikely to be able to earn the purchasing power for consuming at the level they may desire. Adolescents whose families cannot or will not supply them with cash and possessions are fearful of being left out, defeated by those peers who can out-consume them. The desperation of girls is more intense; they are less employable than boys.

These young women are also experiencing the general ambiguity of adolescence, in which there is no clear demarcation between immaturity and maturity. The effort of adolescents to define themselves and to establish an identity separate from parents is a part of normal development, in which conflict is almost inevitable. What is acceptable behavior is usually unclear to both parent and child. What is critical to the future of the adolescent is the form separation from parents takes.

Young women who involve themselves in prostitution often make a definitive and bold psychological and physical rift; they run away. Some are thrown out of their homes, others are abandoned. A few, particularly the deprived, remain at home, but most parental control is relinquished. Running away has become a phenomenon of youth clearly associated with entrance into juvenile prostitution.

The hippie movement of the 1960s and early 1970s validated fleeing parental authority as acceptable problem-solving behavior. In a political attempt to create a counter-culture, a youthful street culture of "flower children" flourished. Street culture did manage to sustain runaways minimally, through a system of "diggers," crash houses, and charity. It was also open to all ethnic groups and economic classes. As the political fervor of the 1960s faded, the symbols of the activists became the substance of a "teeny bopper" culture; a young and apolitical crowd of confused children who had turned to the streets. Juveniles had absorbed and ritualized only the superficialities of non-conformity.

Today many adolescents see running away as a romantic and glamorous solution to their problems, offering them adventure and excitement, as well as independence and escape. Juveniles know that there is at least this alternative to staying in their homes or remaining in placements until they are emancipated or turn eighteen.

Juveniles see other friends and school peers who are "on the run" maintaining themselves with some success. They soak up the exciting stories of independent life. In addition, adolescents know that there are places to go such as hostels and youth shelters which will provide the necessities. Pin ball alleys and fast food shops where juveniles congregate are well known. It is easy to meet people and to find what you need, whether that may be a place to stay or a way to make some easy money. Adolescents know where to run.

Running away can be an occasional, temporary, or permanent remedy to a stressful situation. Running away may mean disappearing to another state, or it may mean leaving home only for the weekend, to go downtown. In either instance, the support systems exist informally, so that the idea of running away is no more improbable for some young people today than going to the prom was two decades ago.

Running away is also an answer to loneliness. The youth street culture is well enough defined to provide a social support network, as well as resources for physically maintaining oneself. The members of the culture have similar stories; they are angry at the same people, and depressed about the same things. Runaways learn from those who preceded them. Street people often assist runaways, teaching them about the hustlers, the dangers, and the exploiters.

Hitchhiking generally provides the mobility for juveniles "on the run." Unfortunately it often includes a scary and abusive sexual experience. Hitchhiking which culminates in a rape contributes to the runaway's history of abusive experiences, further lessening her sense of self-worth and sexual self-respect.

While "on the run" the adolescent must also find food and shelter. The routine episode is meeting "a guy" on the streets, who tells the anxious and lonely juvenile what she needs to hear. He offers her a place to stay. Invariably, a sexual exchange for food and shelter is made, although the bartering aspect is not an overt act in the young girl's mind yet.

The situations we have discussed above are common experiences for large numbers of adolescents. Independent and even rebellious behavior is a well known aspect of adolescent development. The patterns of such behavior take quite different forms, however. How and why do some adolescent girls expand into deviant behavior, specifically including prostitution?

Drift Into Deviance

Entrance into prostitution can best be understood as a process of drift into deviance. The concept of drift, as put forth by Matza, suggests that the delinquent is not fully committed to a deviant lifestyle. According to Matza, "Drift stands midway between freedom and control. . . . The delinquent transiently exists in limbo between convention and crime."[49] The delinquent literally drifts between criminal and conventional action and, therefore, is only "casually, intermittently and transiently immersed in a pattern of illegal action."[50]

The state of being in drift is caused by "underlying influences." According to Matza these influences "make initiation to delinquency more probable and reduce the chances that an event will deflect the drifter from his [sic] delinquent path."[51] The concept of drift has been used to explain movement into prostitution by James and Vitaliano, as well as by N. Davis.[52]

Davis delineated a three stage process consisting of: 1) drift from promiscuity to first act of prostitution; 2) transitional deviance; and 3) professionalization.[53] Davis argues that drift is precipitated by an internalization of a deviant self-concept in response to "informal labeling, public branding and subsequent stigmatization."[54] Early sexual experience is an important factor in Davis' model. James and Vitaliano present a model for a "drift into redefinition of female identity that provides few alternatives to prostitution."[55] They argue that perceived or forced loss of the positive feminine role due to experiences such as molestation, incest, non-continuing relationships, and abortion or miscarriage, undermines sexual self-respect and advances identification with alternative feminine roles; i.e. the fallen woman.[56] James and Vitaliano agree with Davis in that a loss of status and a shift in sex role position is perceived as a loss of the alternatives available to the good woman.

Another study by Karen Rosenblum, which is based on Lemert's theory of primary and secondary deviance,[57] further demonstrates the relationship of female sexuality and female sex roles to prostitution. As noted earlier, Rosenblum argues that "the transition from non-deviance to deviance within prostitution requires only an exaggeration of the situation experienced as a non-deviant woman." Rosenblum further states that "all women, to the degree to which they reflect contemporary female sex roles, are primary deviants."[58] The shift from primary to secondary deviance depends upon "precipitating factors and aspects of the female sex role conducive to a commitment to prostitution," according to Rosenblum.[59]

That primary deviance is "built into" the female sex role[60] is critical to the arguments of Rosenblum, Davis, James and Vitaliano. Precipitating factors such as the attractions of money, independence, or a persuasive pimp, as listed in the opening literature review, are only secondary causes of entrance into prostitution. Internalization of a deviant self-concept based on a negative sexual self-image (whore) promotes primary deviance and the state of drift.

In the section that follows we will describe conditions, events and reactions that make drift into prostitution possible. In addition, we will discuss the process of commitment to prostitution as a lifestyle.

Deviant Drift

We have used the concept of drift between conventional and deviant behavior, as described by Matza,[61] to explain the deviant drift of adolescent females who become involved in prostitution. The state of drift can be seen as an interactive sequence of related processes, including self-identification as a deviant; acculturation to deviant status; and assimilation to a deviant subculture. Each part of the interactive process represents a stage in increasingly deviant behavior and a closer identification with the subculture of prostitution. Social labeling is an important factor at every stage.

Deviant Self-Identification

In the initial stage, self-identification, a child becomes predisposed towards prostitution by adapting to a negative self-image. It has been convincingly argued that negative sexual experiences may precipitate the development of a deviant self-image and a subsequent lifestyle of prostitution.[62] Sexual exploitation, including molestation, incest, and rape, may leave the child with the feeling that she is "sexually spoiled." Sexually abused children may continue to carry feelings of impurity and inferiority with them.

For other women, a negative sexual self-concept may result from the use of sex as a status tool.[63] Sexual intercourse with subsequent failure of a relationship with the sexual partner can have the same negative impact on sexual self-respect as rape or molestation. In the words of a rather perceptive juvenile prostitute, "I thought he'd love me if I let him do it, but I was wrong, I got used." Unplanned pregnancy, abortion, or contracting a venereal disease may have a similar effect. It becomes increasingly difficult to feel unscarred when depreciating sexual experiences are adding up, particularly if they become public knowledge. An adolescent female may feel used, rejected and victimized, yet responsible for her own negative sexual status. She has been provided, in Matza's words, ". . . matter from which the meaning of deviant identity could be conceived and built."[64]

Prostitution offers a salient case for labeling theory, according to N. Davis, because of the strong social sanctions against sex norm violations by women.[65] If the sexual experience of a woman, including sexual victimization, becomes public knowledge, she may be stigmatized for her involvement in a deviant act. Her sex-role position may shift as she loses status among peers and develops a "reputation" for being loose or easy. The shift in sex-role position lends support to Rosenblum's argument that negative sexual experiences relate to the transition from primary to secondary sexual deviance in women.[66]

In the studies we conducted, statistics on the sexual history of the 138 juvenile female prostitutes interviewed revealed a significant incidence of negative sexual experiences. The average age of first intercourse was twelve and a half. The first sexual partner of 10 percent of the prostitutes was a relative. This was true for only 1 percent of the non-prostitutes interviewed. Of the prostitutes, 37 percent had been molested prior to first intercourse, 17 percent by a relative; and 51 percent had been raped, half more than once. Thirty-eight percent had contracted a venereal disease; 40 percent did not use any contraception; and 40 percent had been pregnant. Nineteen percent had had abortions. Forty percent reported feeling uncomfortable about sex. Many non-prostitutes reported similar negative experiences; however, prostitutes reported a higher incidence of negative experiences in individual histories. For example, a prostitute was often an incest victim, had been raped, and had had an abortion.

Negative sexual experiences are generally compounded by other disruptive and degrading life circumstances. These include family instability, parental abuse and neglect, absent parent, failure in school, placement outside the home, and disappointment in peer relations. In our sample of 138 prostitutes, 64 percent had been placed in foster or receiving homes; 65 percent were not in school; 77.2 percent had been expelled from school, usually for absenteeism. In 61 percent of the cases, the parents were not together.

Acculturation

In this process the adolescent begins to perceive the sex role alternatives available to women. The alternatives have been described as a continuum with the madonna at one end and the whore at the other.[67] It becomes clear to the adolescent that because of her sexual experiences, victimization, or both, she cannot fulfill the good girl image. At some point it sinks in that she is defined more precisely as a whore than as a madonna. Self-discovery of her deviant affiliation is reinforced by labeling from those closest to her. Young women involved in prostitution have been told many times, "You are no better than a prostitute," long before they were on the streets. According to Matza, "To be cast a thief, a prostitute, or more generally a deviant is to further compound and hasten the process of becoming that very thing."[68]

This aspect of the drift process is characterized by feelings of embarrassment, depression, and psychological withdrawal. The adolescent becomes increasingly vulnerable and dysfunctional, as the informal label of bad girl begins to stick. Family relationships are volatile and friendships insecure. Failure in school is followed by truancy and finally dropping out. The adolescent commonly responds to the series of rejections and failures by acquiring a new but equally disturbed group of friends. She will find support from other young women who feel that their sexual self-respect has also been compromised.

The adolescent's identification with a delinquent group is a point of transition into secondary deviance as described by Rosenblum. It is marked by the beginning of criminal and delinquent behavior. The adolescent attempts to resolve feelings of confusion, hostility, depression, and loneliness in patterned ways. Promiscuity is a vain effort at securing permanent love. Shoplifting is a grasp at power. Running away is an attempt to escape from misery, based on the illusion that there is something better to run to. Almost invariably, this complex of behavior brings the young woman to the attention of juvenile justice authorities.

In our sample, the criminal involvement pattern for adolescents involved in prostitution varied very little. The first arrest usually occurred by age fourteen, with shoplifting accounting for 32 percent; running away, 27 percent; prostitution, 18 percent. The second arrest was most often for running away, that offense accounting for 27 percent; followed by prostitution, 24 percent, while shoplifting decreased to 12 percent. The third arrest was most often for prostitution, 24 percent; running away, 18 percent; and shoplifting, 4 percent. Criminal activity in other areas increased with involvement in prostitution, particularly for larceny, carrying a concealed weapon, resisting arrest, and assault.

Drug and alcohol use also tends to increase with involvement in the prostitution subculture. Drug and alcohol use symbolize membership in the subculture; substances are also used to cope with the stress of the profession.

Contact with the juvenile justice system reinforces the previous deviant labeling and promotes exposure of the adolescent to prostitution. It is not unusual for the adolescent prostitute to have developed contacts with other juveniles involved in prostitution, in her school or while "on the run," which facilitates her own involvement. Our study points out, however, that adolescents learn the fundamentals of prostitution and often associate with juvenile pimps and prostitutes while under court jurisdiction. It is in detention, receiving, group and foster homes that juveniles make friends with other prostitutes, receive tutoring, and lay plans for the time when they will again be "on the outs."

The findings of N. Davis and Rosenblum concur with ours. Institutionalization—which occurs frequently, because girls can be incarcerated for being sexually active—reinforces the "drift" towards prostitution in two ways. First, it brings a young girl into "intimate association with sophisticated deviants,"[69] who may give the girl her first impression of prostitution as a viable way of life, and even an exciting and rewarding one. Second, incarceration is a major part of the labeling process. A woman in jail is *ipso facto* "deviant," and whether or not she was convicted of, or even engaged in, prostitution, "the societal reactions to women participating in deviant activities is to assume that they are also, or perhaps only, prostitutes."[70] Being labeled deviant and being assumed to be "no better than a prostitute" may remove some women's inhibitions against involvement in the socially disreputable "fast life."

After being released from detention and placed in a court-approved living situation, juveniles predictably run away to their friends. Back on the street, female adolescents observe others making easy money. They are swayed by their imagined potential and encouraged by friends to join in the games of the fast life. Also, they are constrained by needs. The adolescent about to prostitute perceives prostitution as her only means of surviving while becoming independent of an unsympathetic or abusive family. Her decision may be hastened by her observation that money earned in prostitution can command status and respect on the streets.

The actual event which precipitates an act of prostitution varies. A runaway may barter for food, shelter, and a little cash. During a family or personal crisis, an adolescent may turn to prostituting friends who encourage her to gain her independence by joining them. An affluent adolescent may try the first trick on a dare, for the adventure. Often the first opportunity for prostitution presents itself when a customer approaches a girl on the street and offers her money. Or the girl may "fall in love" with a man who turns out to be a pimp, and who convinces her that "a lady will do anything for her man."

Pimps often fill in where social service agencies fail. The adolescent believes in the fantasies offered by the pimp. He becomes her family, reassuring her that "I'll take care of you." The young girl wants to be loved. The pimp says, "I'll love you like you've never been loved before." The pimp attempts to fulfill every need of the adolescent, "I'll be your mother, father, brother, sister, and friend. You don't need anyone but me." The pimp progressively increases the young woman's dependence upon him, isolates her from conventional life, and encourages a deeper commitment to the deviant lifestyle of prostitution. The final trump is the pimp's promise of confirming the girl's image of herself as a successful female: "I'll make a woman out of you." She does not ask herself or him, "What kind of a woman?" Her satisfaction will not necessarily be shattered by abuse at the hands of a pimp. If she has a history of abuse, her conception of love may be compatible with beatings. "They only hit you because they love you."

It is widely believed that prostitution is most commonly entered through the persuasion of pimps. Certainly the recruiting
efforts of the pimp and the attendant flattery affect a young
girl's feelings about herself, bolstering the confidence she needs
to attempt prostitution. Virtually all the female adolescents in
the James study had been approached by a pimp and asked to
prostitute. A significant number, however, had begun prostituting on their own initiative or with a girlfriend.

Involvement with a pimp is inevitable if a young girl
continues to work on the street for more than a few weeks.
According to one young prostitute, "Every woman out there
has a man no matter what she says." Protection on the street
requires the prostitute's having a man, but the need for emotional support is another prime factor. Because of the deviant
and illegal status of prostitution, the social network of the prostitute is restricted to those who are also involved in the "fast
life." The pimp is a dependable lifeline in the relative isolation
of the subculture.

Matza has pointed out that there is a difference between committing deviant acts and defining oneself as a deviant.[71] Typically, the adolescent does not at first recognize her acts as consti-
tuting prostitution. At some point, however, she begins to realize that the behavior she has adopted signifies that she is a prostitute. In drift, according to Matza, "the subject mediates the
process of becoming."[72] The adolescent's image of a prostitute
turns out to be an accurate portrayal of herself, and she is conscious of the popular views: "If you are a prostitute, that is all
you are," and "Once a prostitute, always a prostitute."

Assimilation

Repeated prostitution forces assimilation into the lifestyle of
prostitution and acceptance of an identity as a prostitute.
Assimilation parallels stage 2 in Davis' model: transitional deviance. This stage most perfectly epitomizes the description of a
delinquent in a state of drift. Self-definition as a prostitute is not
absolute. As Davis argues, "They vacillate between convention-
ality and deviance."[73] There may be numerous verbal commitments to stop, along with attempts to return to school, to go
back home, or to get a straight job. These attempts will generally fail if underlying problems of gender-role conflict and low

self-appraisal have not been resolved.

Secondary causes for failure in the conventional world parallel secondary motivations for entrance into prostitution. Adolescents are afraid of being lonely, and most adolescent prostitutes are reluctant to part from the pimp. They are also in need of money. They have no alternative place to live that is satisfactory to them. They are attracted by the subculture, which offers acceptance and success unavailable to them in the straight world. Involvement with the subculture advances the development of a deviant identity at the same time as it increases commitment to illegal activities for support. Assimilation is indicated by adoption of street argot, body language, and other forms of symbolic communication that imply membership in the subculture. The adolescent not only adopts the behavior of her street counterparts, but absorbs their prevailing values. Her social network will eventually be made up exclusively of street people.

An arrest for prostitution symbolizes formal labeling as a prostitute. In most states, once arrested, a woman takes on the status of a "known prostitute" and is subject to arrest for loitering with the intent of committing an act of prostitution. Sixty percent of our sample were "known prostitutes." Being called a "known prostitute" while still an adolescent obviously provides a young woman with the basis for self-interpretation that is negative and perhaps permanent.

Commitment

Few adolescents who become involved in prostitution actually fully commit themselves to prostitution as a permanent vocation. Maturation and splitting up of the peer group usually contribute to a change in lifestyle.[74] Those who do commit themselves to prostitution have drifted towards the deviant end of the available sexual identity spectrum for women, the whore. It is important to recognize this part of the sequence if intervention is to be effective.

Discussion

Our research suggests that the most important precursor to prostitution for all women consists of sexual experience and conditioning which direct them to define their self-worth in sexual terms. Beginning with early childhood, females are rewarded primarily for being cute, endearing, and giving. They learn to make exchanges, bartering first with personal attractiveness and later with sex. Early physical development, negative sexual experiences, and rewards for attractiveness and passivity reinforce the female's convictions that her value as a human being is measured by the sexual responses she evokes. Adolescent women know that their womanhood, identified by society with their bodies, is salable. The females most at risk are the victims of sexual exploitation and abuse, who suffer the loss of a positive feminine identity.

Puberty intensifies the vulnerability of adolescents to a poor self-image. The junior high level, particularly age twelve, is an especially critical time for girls. Simons, *et. al.*, have argued that vulnerability to a poor self image at this age is due to environmental, social, and physiological changes.[75] At age twelve, adolescents often must change schools and develop a new social network. They face the possibility of rejection by peers; they fear not making it into the "in crowd." The major social change that begins in junior high school is dating. The rules, risks, and rituals of dating contribute to the uncertainty and self-consciousness characteristic of adolescents. The physiological changes associated with puberty are additional factors contributing to instability in the adolescent's self-concept. Adolescents in general, then, are not self-assured. Those who are abused or neglected, or who have undergone other depreciating experiences, are even more defenseless than the general run of adolescents.

Some would argue that "drift" ends with commitment. Consistent with Matza's thesis, however, even the experienced prostitute may have internalized both conventional and fast life norms. N. Davis argues that although sex has become a vocation, and deviance is no longer segmented, reference group orientations and lifestyles vary a great deal among prostitutes.[76] The continuation of drift is also demonstrated by recurring plans to quit the profession.

The deviant identity of an adolescent woman involved in prostitution is supported by an interactive social process.

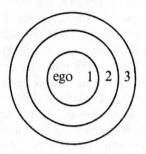

1. self-identification
2. informal labeling
3. societal reaction and formal sanction

Initially ego discovers that her self-image is congruent with her learned perception of a deviant woman. The deviant self-image is reinforced through labeling by those closest to her in her social network. Her response is to behave appropriately to the role in which she has been cast. She does not perceive any available alternatives for a woman with her status. A societal reaction to her behavior follows, with formal labeling as a prostitute and periodic institutionalization. As interactions accumulate, the woman may be forced in the direction of commitment. Institutionalization and the juvenile justice system are held liable for providing incentive for drift into illegal behavior and a commitment to deviance by Matza, Davis and Rosenblum. Each interaction with the system advances deviant labeling, and prepares the adolescent for the next encounter by conditioning her for increased sanctions. The conception of drift and female juvenile prostitution is compatible with Bandura's formulation of the self-system in which psychological functioning is viewed as the reciprocally determined outcome of behavioral, cognitive, and environmental influences.[77]

Intervention

Self-interpretation as a deviant woman is amplified by informal and formal labeling. Messages to the contrary must permeate three layers of negative identification. Each layer—formal labeling, informal labeling, and self-perception—acts as a barrier that a prostitute must mediate, if she is to succeed in redefining herself. Helping the juvenile prostitute to re-evaluate her cognitive perceptions in light of past sexual labeling by herself and others, rather than institutionalizing her, may exert a positive effect on her feelings and future behavior.[78]

Our experience with juvenile prostitutes has shown sex-role counseling to be much more effective than job training, employment, or institutionalization (unless protection from sexual abuse is necessary). These young women have often been unable to change their response patterns because they have perceived alternate feminine roles as unattainable. Without informed counseling, they have been unable to recognize the differences between their perception of themselves as sexual offenders and their probable status as sexual victims.

Sex-role counseling has three goals: 1) to restore and expand the juvenile's concept of successful feminine roles; 2) to alter the effect of labeling and the permanence of that label; and 3) to help juveniles recognize the difference between their perceptions of themselves as sexual offenders and their status as sexual victims.[79]

Conclusion

Most prostitution research has probed such factors as early neglect and economic impetus, but not the perceived or forced loss of a female's self-esteem. Our research indicates that such loss is an important factor. The potential effects of labeling and the perceived permanence of that label must also be seriously examined. "Once a whore, always a whore" is a sentiment often expressed by prostitutes who were stigmatized during adolescence. Counseling of sexually abused juveniles should be informed by awareness of the pejorative effects of early loss of self-esteem coupled with labeling. This population of young women needs intervention aimed at restoring and expanding their concepts of successful feminine roles in contemporary society.

The Politics of Sexual Assault
Facing the Challenge

Sandra Butler

When I began my research in 1975 into the genesis of incestuous assault, the commonly held theoretical and clinical opinion was that it was a rare occurrence, perhaps happening to one in a million girls, and usually within lower-class rural or fragmented inner city families. Over the past ten years, as more women began to come forward to report their abuses and more sophisticated screening and intake procedures were developed in youth serving agencies, evidence of the incidence has increased quite drastically. In alcohol abuse programs, runaway shelters, chemical dependency centers and counseling programs for prostitutes (all barometers of a female population in pain, enraged and powerless), it began to appear that sexual abuse was not something that happened to one child in a million. Rather, it began to be clear that incestuous assault and its concomitant—profound betrayal of children by adults, loss of emotional safety, and abrupt interruption of the maturation process—were widespread.

In a recently completed study of sexually abused prostitutes, the following corroborative statistics were gathered. Ninety percent of this population lost their virginity through sexual assault; 91 percent felt there was no one to tell and nothing they could do; 1 percent spoke with a professional; and 3 percent reported their assault to the police. Ninety-six percent reported that the assault affected their decision to run away, and 70 percent reported that it affected their decision to prostitute. Among the total number of women studied, 61 percent of the assaults were incestuous and only 10 percent were by strangers.[1] These figures verify findings of other, similar studies being done across the country, confirming the patterns of early sexual abuse, most often by a trusted male adult within the family setting.[2]

This new statistical information indicates that all of our previous theoretical analyses were based on a central misconception: that incestuous assault is something that happens in very rare circumstances, in very rare families, and is perpetrated by very unusual men. This misconception has been augmented both by the low reporting rate of victims and by reluctance on the part of many people to accept the validity of the reports when they are made. Additionally, the silence and denial of two of the most influential sexual theorists and researchers of our time has affected theory, clinical training, and public response to this problem. The first of these major theorists was Freud, who chose to disbelieve his patients' reports of sexual assaults by their fathers rather than face the implications of the behavior of his friends and peers.[3] The second was Kinsey, who failed to publish his findings on the sexual assault of children.[4]

Now that professional silences are being broken and more children are being identified as victims of sexual abuse, our theory has begun to change under the pressure of changing statistics. It is inevitable that our new awareness that this phenomenon is of epidemic proportions should inform our judgments and that clinicians are beginning to reconstruct theoretical analyses in light of the newly available facts.

One direct consequence of increased reporting is that it has become more difficult in the face of such overwhelming evidence to disbelieve what our children are telling us. Freud's denial and disbelief were based not simply on bad faith but on bad facts. A second consequence of the changing information is that the stereotypical portraits of the rural patriarchal figure who sexually abuses his daughters or the poor urban father suffering from myriad kinds of stress are falling into disrepute. Those reassuring and distancing images are being dispelled by reports of abuse by nearly every kind of man, from every race, class, religious affiliation and state of mind. The sexual assault of children has been observed in agrarian communities, as well as in highly industrialized cities and suburbs which include all permutations of class, race, and nationality. The myths die hard, of course, for they serve several functions, not the least of which is the maintenance of the sexual *status quo*.

Myth vs. Fact

I have elsewhere discussed these self-contradictory myths.[5] To review quite briefly they are as follows:

Young girls are seductive.

Young girls are not seductive, but they make up stories of assault to express anger at adults.

Mothers know about the assault but do not act to protect their children.

Mothers do not know about the assault but cause it to happen because they do not maintain their role as sexual, emotional, psychological, and nurturing caretakers in the family.

Fathers are sick perverts (lower-class assault).

Fathers are stress-filled men who are expressing inappropriate love to their daughters (middle-class assault).

Families are systems in which the assault is used to maintain emotional balance.

Incest is rare.

Incest is not rare and perhaps therefore not so damaging to the child.

Incest is a rite of passage useful for the child's development into a successful womanhood.

Incest itself is not damaging. The trauma is caused by the response of an overly puritanical and sexually anxious society.

Incest is quite damaging and causes frigidity, prostitution and lesbianism (all making a woman unfit for a monogamous, heterosexual and silently acquiescent marriage).

Present-day fact gathering and analysis refute this conglomeration of myths. What we are discovering is that incestuous assault is almost always visited upon young female children by adult males. Almost always, it is a male who is in a position of power and authority over the child, in terms of relationship as well as of age and size. Almost always, it is a male who has the trust of the child and access to her in her own home, often in her own bed. The homes and beds in which these violations occur are not confined to remote mountain communities, or to third world or poor white families. The incidents are not rare, nor do they occur more rarely in middle- and upper-class families. They are not willful fabrications by children; and they are not precipitated by the child's sexual longing and seductive behavior. Incest is not the product of passive encouragement by the child's mother. Finally, female children do not learn anything useful about becoming a woman from the experience of incestuous assault—unless so flagrant an abuse of power can be seen as an object lesson of woman's oppression and victimization.

Myths about incestuous assault have provided a smoke screen for the social, psychological, and political conditions which are at its actual root. For incest is the imposition of power by an adult seeking to satisfy his own needs, whether sexual, emotional, or pathological. The child is present in the flesh, but in the flesh only. She is a stand-in for the fantasies that are projected onto her small being, out of the male's insecurity, fear, or anger. The child's needs are not taken into account, the developmental damage to her life is not considered. Her fear and isolation are the prices that must be paid in order for the adult male to satisfy his inner promptings.

Shortcomings of Conventional Approaches

Unfortunately, the clinical interventions and analyses that have been developed to date have been based on the mythology of assault rather than its actual dynamics. Consequently, when the still relatively rare report is made, the child who was victimized is most often removed from her home. The child's mother is typically placed in the position of being forced to choose between believing, protecting, and defending her child and protecting and defending her husband; often, through fear of male aggression or social and economic consequences, she chooses the latter.

The approach of many conventional therapists to these cases has been a systematic exploration of the childhood and adult life of male offenders. Their findings, with surprising consistency, have led to the identification of a variety of people and forces responsible in one way or another for leading the offender to commit his assault. The implicated persons are frequently female. For instance, the offender's mother has been observed as too passive, too aggressive, offering both too much love and too little. His wife has been described as passive in some studies, and withholding and cold in others. His daughter is described as unable to protect herself, desirous of the assault, anxious to use it as a way to manipulate her situation, and so on. Nearly every perspective is presented *except* that of an adult man taking advantage of his superior size, strength, and male authority to enforce a child's obedience to his needs and wishes.

Some clinicians and social workers go beyond a primary focus on the male incestuous offender to a closer examination of the family as a unit. Again, however, usually all variables are explored *except* male dominance in the family, in society, and in the economic marketplace. Most commonly, the investigation of family dynamics centers on patterns of communication between husband and wife, expectations in choice of a marital partner, sexual, emotional, and work-related stresses upon the male, wifely inability or unwillingness to nurture. Not surprisingly, the inadequacies of the female marriage partner are often identified as a causative factor in the male's incestuous assault.

In short, almost all approaches to incestuous assault ignore the fundamental problem of an imbalance and abuse of power: by men over women, and by adults over children. While there are multiple factors in incestuous assault which require research, analysis, and explication, it is this neglected area which most urgently needs to be addressed. For incestuous assault is overwhelmingly the assault of female children by adult males; it takes place on a large scale; and—it is against the law. It is important that a feminist analysis take precedence over other interpretations, since it is an analysis which encompasses all existing theories and examines them in the realistic context of gender relations.

When Is a Law Not a Law?

Such an analysis is necessary for an understanding of law enforcement practices, as well as for developing appropriate intervention strategies. As a society, we have little trouble in perceiving that a law has been broken when a store is robbed; but much confusion arises when the object of violation is a child's body. Even if there is awareness that law is being violated—the law we have developed, as a society, to protect the bodies and lives of children—there is great reluctance to make the arrests and prosecutions necessary to maintain a standard of law, either because of fear of "family disintegration" or for fear of adding another family to the welfare rolls. There is a premature rush to believe the protestations of the immediately penitent aggressor. Would we respond similarly to an apologetic car thief who might plead that loss of his job caused dire stress on his pocketbook and his family's needs? Assuredly, we would not. Why and how has a car come to be considered more valuable than a body belonging to a child? Such contrasting responses offer a revealing comment not only on societal values, but on the politics of sexual assault.

While various programs are now in existence around the country, they are frequently developed from a perspective that is apolitical or politically conventional. My own view is that to be effective, programs on sexual assault must consciously embrace the issues of male power and sexual privilege and be directed toward increasing the empowerment of women and children. Some few programs of this kind are presently in operation.

Model Programs

The treatment model represented by the Sexual Abuse Center at Harborview Hospital in Seattle, Washington and the prevention program designed by the Child Assault Prevention Project (CAP) sponsored by Women Against Rape in Columbus, Ohio are two of the best examples of visionary and effective work.[6]

In Seattle, if a child or neighbor reports suspected sexual abuse, there is a systematized community response of full scope, which follows clear and consistent procedures. The child is believed and supported. The father is, when possible, removed from the home. The mother is given immediate homemaker assistance and legal and social service aid. Testimony is gathered from the child by a specially trained team of investigators who represent the departments appropriate to intervention in various aspects of the case. As warranted by evidence, prosecution is encouraged. There is no moralizing or ethical confusion. The primary focus is on the child victim, and the message to the assailant is clear and uncompromising. "What you did is perverted, damaging to the child, and against the law. We as a community are outraged and you will have to pay a price." In many cases this means a carefully structured program which incorporates behavior modification techniques and counseling for aggressors. In other cases, depending on the nature of the assault and the assailant's response to his arrest, he is sent to a locked facility. The child participates in on-going groups that are well-supervised by staff, and her real situation is the basis from which all counseling work flows.

In Columbus, Ohio, an important pilot prevention project, offered by CAP through the schools, teaches children what they need to know to be "safe, strong, and free." Women trained in crisis intervention for victims of sexual assault take responsibility for classroom role playing and the discussion that follows. Role-playing situations include peers, strangers, and family members. Each role play is repeated twice. Parents as well as classroom teachers are directly involved in the program, in order to prepare them for providing children with an on-going source of information and support. Through learning specific techniques for recognizing, avoiding, or fighting back against attempted assault, and through the identification of a support system within the school and in the larger community, children are able to gain a greater sense of control over their bodies and their lives. While some similar programs exist elsewhere, CAP is unique for its grounding in a feminist understanding of the child's powerlessness and dependency, coupled with a deep respect for children.

But it is not enough for us to have a feminist analysis, or a few outstanding examples of effective programs, or meticulous social scientists gathering data and interpreting them carefully. It is also not enough to have, in each community, a few well trained women to do the painful and important therapeutic work with the victims of sexual assault. For the sheer volume of cases demands that we seek out augmented resources and a deepened response to the needs.

I would recommend that women return to the earliest techniques of the contemporary feminist movement, applying the insights and skills of consciousness-raising to programs dealing with sexual assault. In the hands of the growing number of women trained as feminist counselors, group leaders, psychotherapists, and social workers, that early approach can bring our work and our political vision closer together. While I will briefly and generally recapitulate that approach here, more specific applications and new transformations would evolve from particular community needs, skills, population, and cultural demography.

Consciousness-raising Revisited

One of the earliest movement handbooks, *Free Space*, by Pam Allen, described the deliberate organizing of all-female groups in which women could come together to discuss issues of importance to their lives. The feeling of safety in bearing witness to our lives among other women cannot be achieved quite so well under any other circumstances. Although the details of individual experience may differ, the similarities have been found overwhelming. And the awareness that evolves out of shared lives and a shared understanding is powerful, allowing women to begin moving away from emotionally privatized lives of silence, self-blame and guilt.

Women are, indeed, beginning to come together now to talk about their experiences of sexual assault—in some cases, assaults that occurred ten years, twenty years, half-a-lifetime past. For most, it is the first time that they have felt safe in speaking, have felt that they are heard and believed. For most, these sessions represent the beginning of recognition that the phenomenon of sexual assault is not an individual problem unique to themselves. For nearly all, there is a growing appreciation of the strength and resourcefulness that have been required of them, in order to survive in a world which denies the realities of their lives. Theories of incestuous assault which have centered on alleged female submissiveness, masochism, and seduction are at radical odds with the realities of women's experience of assault. Coming together, women realize that they are the primary source of information, the best experts on the subject. Feminist theory is based upon facts gathered in this manner, facts which are rooted in the common experience and the common oppression of women and children.

What is beginning to happen on a small scale in some communities across the country is that women are turning away from the clinicians who base their work on theories of subconscious "feminine" motivations as causative factors: seduction, sexual desire, hostility, manipulation. The alternative to such clinical practice, many women are discovering, is the intimate self-help group.

While it is a small step, this discovery is crucial in the lives of the women participants. Moreover, some of the women will be able to use this on-going work as a base from which to grow. A collective-called Pleides, for example, formed in San Francisco, is now being replicated in other major cities. Pleides members have made presentations to women's gatherings and have offered themselves as resources for on-going support groups, private referrals, public education, and political organizing. Pleides' services have been eagerly sought; there is, at this writing, a long waiting list of women wanting guidance in forming groups of various kinds. The bonding, in short, has begun to occur. In the six years of my own work, I have seen the silence beginning to break, women beginning to join together to understand the commonalities of their assault, their responses to it, the struggles they have had in trying to grow into strong and autonomous human beings. This nascent work of organizing cannot be underestimated. I can remember similar meetings of no more than thirty people in New York, beginning to explore ways of developing teach-ins to discuss the reality of the escalating Vietnam War. I can also remember meetings of less than twenty discussing ways to organize the first public demonstration on Fifth Avenue against the war. And from those small yet powerful seeds, major structural change can proceed. For once the first group of women has begun, others can build upon the framework they provide, forming groups that reflect their own community needs. And as the movement grows, the tens of thousands of women who need to speak and to be heard can find a place in the structure we build together, and can begin to heal.

From Private Healing to Public Impact

This is the beginning of our gathering the raw material of our lives together in a safety that does not impale us further on judgment, harsh analysis, and self-blame. As this movement spreads from the small self-help peer support group, we can begin to broaden our scope by drawing in those within the women's community who have skills and training as therapists, social workers, child protective workers, criminal justice personnel, and political organizers. As we incorporate professional women with a feminist perspective on the issue of sexual assault, we can strike the important balance between individual healing and public and institutional change. The foundation will be laid for increasing public awareness that women and children are the responsibility of the entire social community, and that they have an absolute right to safety, dignity, and freedom from any form of tyranny and abuse, whether it be physical, emotional, or sexual. As we continue to organize, we can train teachers not just to allow but to encourage children to tell them about their troublesome experiences, in their own words. We must continue to learn, and to teach, openness to children and sympathetic belief in them. As we grow we can create safe houses for women and children who are at risk in their own homes. We can create more shelters for adolescents, to which they can go in utter confidentiality, where youth-oriented medical and legal counseling will be available. Such places will require women trained as advocates, able to guide sexually abused children through whatever rehabilitative or legal processes their situations call for. In these protected environments, offering practical assistance and emotional support, damaged young people can develop self-esteem as well as trust in others.

We can achieve sufficient strength to insist on the development of educational programs in our schools that will teach our children the truth about their bodies and their right to say no to anyone who uses their bodies in ways that they feel are bad or unacceptable. We can begin to lobby in our civic groups, our places of worship, our community mental and physical health centers, our social agencies, for programs reflecting genuine concern for children, adolescents, and women. The victims among these groups who have and will find the courage to speak out provide impetus for the rest of us. And as feminists we can conduct realistic, on-going evaluation of the intervention systems, treatment techniques, and resources developed in our communities, while continuing to serve as community educators and organizers.

We are still at the earliest stages of this effort. Like all first steps, it requires courage, particularly of those women, so long silent, who are now sharing the truths of their lives with us. But by adding our voices to theirs and grasping the political tools which lie at hand, we can begin to break the historic patterns of sexual violence.

Advocacy for Teenage Women in the Justice System
One Model for Change

Sue Davidson

Young people who come into conflict with the law are frequently referred to as "troubled youth." Over the decades since the first juvenile court was established in 1899, there has been a body of opinion supporting the view that the youths of this country are not nearly so "troubled" as a legal system which punishes them, in shocking numbers, often for no more than the conditions of being young and of springing from poor and working-class families, in many cases of minority race.[1] The thesis that the juvenile justice system may be at least as troubled as those it processes is especially persuasive as it applies to female juvenile offenders. Evidence is accumulating that young women offenders, historically and in present times, are punished not only for their youth and for their social, ethnic, and economic backgrounds, but also for their gender.[2]

An avenue for redressing the legal abuse of both sexes was opened by the passage in 1974 of the Juvenile Justice and Delinquency Prevention Act. In its emphasis upon reforming practices inappropriate to noncriminal offenders—such as their incarceration—the act was significant for youth generally; but it was of special significance for the female juvenile court population, among whom such a very small percentage are charged with criminal offenses.[3] To further the goals of deinstitutionalizing youthful offenders and to support improvements in all services to these youth, the Juvenile Justice Amendments of 1977 provided for youth advocacy programs. Among the programs funded under the new provisions in 1979 was the National Female Advocacy Project, based in Tucson, Arizona.[4] Because it is the only federally funded project in the country focused entirely on promoting the interests of young women affected by the juvenile justice system, it provides a unique model for advocacy on behalf of this group.

Background of the Project

The National Female Advocacy Project was not an instant birth. It had its origins in advocacy activities already well established in its parent organization, New Directions for Young Women, Tucson, to which the federal grant was awarded. By 1978, two years after its founding, New Directions was credited as the force responsible for near-elimination of the practice of detaining female status offenders in Pima County, with the support of the juvenile court's already highly progressive presiding judge, as well as that of the court administrator and others within the juvenile court center.[5] This accomplishment and others benefitting girls were the results of New Directions' own imaginative direct services to young women, its cultivation of augmented services from other community sources, and its aggressive program of public education and cooperative action with a broad range of private and governmental agencies.

New Directions has used the federal grant to intensify its advocacy programs in Arizona and in the added demonstration state of Oregon, and to expand advocacy efforts nationally. The goals of the project at every level—local, state, and national—are to effect changes that will overcome neglect of young women or outright discrimination against them in laws, in the institutional policies and practices of courts, police, schools, health and welfare agencies, and in specific programs offered by private and public youth-serving agencies.

The National Female Advocacy Project's approach to these monumental goals bears a good many earmarks of classic, American-style social action campaigns for the advancement of causes or groups lacking power in the society. Ruth Crow, until recently on the administrative staff of the Pima County Juvenile Court Center, and now the Advocacy Project's director, is a richly-experienced veteran of the peace, civil rights, and feminist movements. She was the prime mover behind New Directions for

Young Women, soon joined by Carol Zimmerman, who became that organization's executive director. Zimmerman, by profession a nurse, is also a women's rights activist. Unlike a good many persons working in direct services, these two women had no difficulty in distinguishing between advocacy for individual clients and the advocacy intended by the 1977 congressional amendments, aimed at system changes. With their small, all-female staff increased to a total of nine project workers, they knew where to begin, what needed to be done, and a great deal about how to go about doing it.[6]

How the Project Works

The project's approach is two-pronged, aimed at educating relevant groups (as, teachers, counselors, corrections personnel) to the issues affecting the lives of young females, and at mobilizing concerned individuals and groups to press for needed changes in the juvenile justice, social service, and educational systems. In the initial mobilizing phases, the project's strategy has been roughly the same at the national as at the state levels. The project has looked for its opening wedges among groups which are "natural" allies; first and foremost, organizations with a pre-existing commitment to the rights and welfare of women and children. Work in Arizona and Oregon differs from work at the national level in the relatively greater opportunities for state-level workers to reach beyond the "natural" allies and bring more peripheral interest groups into the common effort, as well as to put direct pressure upon the law and policy makers accessible at the local and state levels. The main thrust of the project nationally is to persuade its "natural" organizational allies to put young female offenders' problems on their action agendas. The intensive work must then be pursued by those organizations and their own state and local affiliates; however, the National Female Advocacy Project offers them a growing wealth of resources on which to draw in this effort: fact sheets on such subjects as employment, sexual abuse, and sexuality as these affect the lives of young women; published results of a slowly accumulating body of research by feminist scholars; general recommendations for public policy changes; information on model alternatives to incarceration of the young; education and training materials for sensitizing youth workers to issues of sex, class, and race; a national roster of speakers and group trainers; and consultants from among the advocacy project's own staff.

It was not until 1979 that Crow and Zimmerman began to travel a national circuit, making their appeal for young women at a variety of social welfare and women's conferences from coast to coast. As early as 1977, however, they had laid the groundwork for gaining these platforms, as the chief organizers of a national conference, "Changing Values: Teenage Women in the Juvenile Justice System," held in Tucson. Jointly sponsored by the Pima County Juvenile Justice Collaboration, New Directions for Young Women, and the Pima County Juvenile Court, the event drew participants and nationally known speakers from throughout the United States. Conference participants may have wondered, upon their arrival, what they were all doing there together, for they seemed at first an oddly assorted lot. Scholars in women's studies sat down to lunch with parole officers and Campfire Girls group leaders; judges and legislators mingled in the hallways with vocal feminist and Third World political activists; legal theoreticians, high school teachers, directors of runaway shelters, fundraisers for rape relief centers made one another's acquaintance in front of the literature table, tended by blue-jeaned volunteers from the local women's book store, who also joined in the conversations. It was, as one social worker from Washington State remarked, "some crew." By the time the conference ended, two days later, the participants had a much better grasp of the reasons for their having been brought together. The essential concept, explained by Ruth Crow, had penetrated. "We want the people who deal directly with youth to get a feminist perspective on the problems they're seeing. Just as urgently, we want to make feminist scholars and activists *see* this population of wronged young women and to make them a special consideration, as they have not so far done. It will take the expertise and cooperation of all of them to make an impact on the climate of opinion, on lawmakers, on the institutions that shape children's lives."

Cooperation with National Groups

Through contacts nourished since the 1977 conference, and with the financial assistance of the advocacy grant, the project is now doing its best to make the population of wronged young women visible to groups around the country. National engagements have been secured primarily with organizations which focus on youth or women, but these represent a spectrum from grassroots groups (e.g., Women for Racial and Economic Equality), to highly political associations (e.g., National Organization for Women), to professional organizations that are well established on the American scene (e.g., National Council of Juvenile and Family Court Judges). The effectiveness of the project's national outreach may be measured by the growing volume of requests for speakers and materials, and by the beginning of that serious commitment of resources the project hopes to generate within the organizations themselves. For example, the national Girls Clubs of America, Inc., already a leader in improving services to young women, has responded enthusiastically by co-sponsoring with the project a series of regional forums aimed at promoting changes in systems affecting girls in conflict with the law. In another instance, the National Council of Jewish Women, as the result of a seminar with the project, formed a task force on young women in the juvenile justice system and developed recommendations for addressing the issues, which it has disseminated to its local chapters. The council furthermore submitted to the Lowe Foundation a proposal to study the conditions of adolescent girls in the justice system. It was awarded a grant for this research, which represents perhaps the first comprehensive attempt to gather national data on the subject.[7]

Information, Literature, and Training

Requests to the project for information, advice, and literature also come from a large number and variety of public agencies, as well as occasional invitations to the platforms of official bodies. In Boston, a project representative presented a paper, a workshop, and policy recommendations on the employment needs of young women to the 1980 Vice-Presidential Task Force on Youth Employment. In Ocala, Florida, the project gave a day-and-a-half workshop on the female status offender under the auspices of the Southeastern Correctional Management Council. In Racine, Wisconsin, advocacy staff met with fifty Wisconsin policy makers and program administrators at an intensive two-day planning conference on "Today's Young Women in Wisconsin," sponsored by the State Department of Health and Social Services. One outcome was a "critical issues and needs" statement, together with enlightened recommendations on female offenders. A statewide task force was formed to pursue the goals of "making these recommendations a reality."[8]

Intensive Work in Arizona and Oregon

While the project works nationally to stimulate such developments, its Arizona and Oregon offices are heavily and intimately involved in the day-to-day work of gathering facts on the condition of females in the juvenile justice and social service systems of those states, of focusing attention on needed institutional changes, of monitoring proposed legislation affecting young women and providing expert testimony, of identifying and cooperating with other concerned groups, agencies, and individuals, of helping to build state and local coalitions of like-minded groups. It is at the state level, too, that the project has begun a program for training young women to become advocates for their peers. Volunteers for this program, recruited from youth organizations, drawn from clients using New Directions' own direct services, or attracted by news stories about the project, will gain experience, information, and skills enabling them to participate in all aspects of the project's work.

The project's work in Arizona and Oregon is both more immediately rewarding and more frustrating than the national work. In the relatively small theatre of state operations, it is less difficult than at the national level to make contacts and form relationships with a multiplicity of organizations and agencies, to attend the regular meetings of private groups and public bodies, to gain visibility and trust, and even to attain a degree of status and power. It is all the more disheartening when, having penetrated so far, the mission gets stuck at some mid-point short of satisfactory outcomes.

The array of organizations and agencies with which the state offices cooperate encompasses a diversity of elements: "mainstream" organizations such as the League of Women Voters and the Girl Scouts; ethnic advancement associations ranging from the long-established Urban League to the more recent El Rio Neighborhood Health Center; self-help and "people's" groups, such as La Frontera Mental Health Center, Tucson Youth Council, Portland (Oregon) Area Citizens for Children, Center for Social Change; juvenile justice and youth professionals, such as the Oregon Youth Workers Alliance and the Arizona Council of Attorneys for Children; public bodies such as the Oregon Children's Services Division and the Arizona Department of Economic Security. The project's state offices are in close touch with groups devoted to women's rights and welfare, from officially appointed women's commissions to independently organized women's political caucuses—and every organized effort in-between. The Arizona and Oregon projects are also members of various broad-based coalitions concerned with women and youth, such as the Oregon Women's Rights Coalition and the Pima County Collaboration for Children and Youth.

"I hope to shock you today—to make you feel a bit of anger and outrage." The speaker was Annie Taylor, director of the advocacy project's Oregon office; and she was addressing the legislature's House Interim Committee on Human Resources. She went on to observe that while the goal of equal rights for women has made some progress, yet in the juvenile justice system to date, "women are perceived as either madonnas or whores and treated accordingly." The expressive style of Janet Marcotte, project director of the Arizona office, is lower-key, but no less insistent. Regardless of style, however, and regardless of the boat-rocking content of their public messages, neither of these women can be dismissed as "outside agitators." Taylor serves on a list of home-grown boards and councils (from Girl Scouts to Mid-Valley Center against Domestic and Sexual Violence), as does Marcotte, a long-time child welfare advocate, and currently president of the Arizona Foundation for Children. Moreover, the projects they direct are anchored firmly in the network of indigenous organizations and agencies already indicated.

Sometimes alone, more often in the company of allies, Arizona and Oregon advocacy workers attack issues crucial to the fate of female youth. Paramount among these is implementation of the Juvenile Justice and Delinquency Prevention Act's initiative to remove juveniles from locked facilities and provide positive alternatives to detention. In Oregon, which has a poor record of compliance with the Act, the project's investigations revealed that of females held in detention centers and jails in 1979, 60 percent were charged with non-criminal offenses. The project is working to broaden options to incarceration of these female status offenders, an effort which inevitably embroils it in struggles for public funding for non-coercive, community-based services. At the same time, the project attempts to influence the inequitable provisions for females at the state training school, such as the school's severely limited, sex-stereotyped vocational training offerings. Studies of girls' services in Oregon were undertaken by statewide task forces brought together by the advocacy project. This independent effort sparked the formation of an official Girls Program Study Committee by the state's Children's Services Division—an entity with which the project is half the time at loggerheads, half the time in harmony. At any rate, the project considered its own appointment to the new committee a "bureaucratic victory." The CDS subsequently followed through with a workshop aimed at implementing new services for young women and at increasing the 1981 state budget specifically for girls. It also accepted a project proposal for sex-awareness training of its own managers and program staff. This kind of co-operation, while it assures no ultimate successes, at least strengthens the institutional base of the project's support. The project also maintains a friendly but not altogether easy relationship with the State Department of Education. For example, while the department agrees with the project's position that state-mandated child care should be available to teenage parents attempting to continue their education, it does not wish to be responsible for this care, preferring that it be handled by the Children's Services Division. Even while project staff was trekking back and forth between the two state agencies in search of a solution to this obstinate problem, the Department of Education was assisting in the planning of a statewide conference on teenage pregnancy and teen parents, which it co-sponsored with the female advocacy project and a number of other Oregon associations.

In Arizona, advocacy staff regularly visits officials in a variety of government agencies, both in order to secure information on the status of programs for young women and to suggest programs appropriate to young women's needs. Often, having made a persuasive case for a specific need, the advocacy project supplies the resources to fill it. For example, the project early-on established contacts with the Southern Arizona office of the Department of Economic Security, pressing the need to sensitize personnel in rural areas to the special problems faced by young women. The office responded by co-sponsoring with the project a series of staff training workshops in four rural Arizona locations. Similarly, the project conducted workshops on sexual stereotyping with adult personnel and youth in the Manpower *(sic)* Youth Program, and provided training to Tucson Job Corps staff, as a result of which, educational materials on women and work were incorporated into the SAJC's overall program. Following successful seminars on sexuality with Papago youth, the project was invited to present a workshop in cooperation with the Papago CETA* Youth Project, attended by over a hundred Papago Indian community organizers.

In Arizona as in Oregon, the project is immersed in legislative work. Project staff, for example, coordinated youth advocacy efforts for the Juvenile Justice Task Force of the Arizona Legislative Council during the 1981 legislative session. The project has also undertaken selective individual advocacy, in a case of public consequence for female youth. In the Nogales trial of a guard accused of sexually assaulting a young woman imprisoned as a runaway from another state, project staff acted in an advisory capacity, supplying the girl's attorney with analytical and statistical data. Staff members of New Directions and its advocacy project also provided emotional support to the young woman in a generally hostile environment. The guard was found guilty and sentenced to six months in jail and three years' probation. The case was well covered by the press, bringing public attention to the victimization of teenage females in the juvenile justice system, as well as serving notice that such abuses are under scrutiny. In the wake of the affair, the project received numerous requests to continue female advocacy efforts in Nogales.

While the Nogales court decision is among the more tangible effects of the project's efforts, there are other concrete outcomes, as in the ongoing struggles over state and local funding. In company with other children's advocates in Oregon, the project held back severe retrenchments in the 1980 budget for the Juvenile Services Commission, winning a battle to reduce the Governor's proposed cut of 63 percent to 30 percent. In Arizona, project workers and a host of collaborators managed to wrest from the City of Tucson's 1981 budget an additional $100,000 for

* Comprehensive Employment and Training Act

general social services.

Collaborative efforts aimed directly at preventing youth from being locked up, however, have not fared well in either Arizona or Oregon. Impact on state legislation is as yet unsatisfactory; and juvenile court practices in many jurisdictions are a long way from improving. In Pima County, where the project was born, it immediately faced a quickly changing situation with the appointment of a new presiding juvenile court judge whose philosophy on status offenders differs sharply from her predecessor's. Arizona project director Janet Marcotte reported at a legislative committee hearing that Pima County Juvenile Court statistics showed a 99 percent increase between 1978–1979 in the number of young people detained. In the first three months of 1980, girls accounted for 60 percent of the youth detained for status offenses, while comprising only 23 percent of all young people held in detention.

Toward the Future

These are, of course, discouraging facts. Yet project workers did not expect to produce instant, irreversible changes in systems long entrenched in the society, or suddenly erase the deeply ingrained prejudices which support practices inimical to young women. "We have accomplished much that we set out to do," says project director Ruth Crow. "We have exposed facts, we have raised awareness of the discriminatory attitudes and practices which injure females in the juvenile justice system—largely the poor and racial minorities—and we have set in motion groups and individuals who were not moving on these particular issues before. That hasn't brought the injuries to a halt. But I'd say it's a beginning."

Scarcely off the ground, the National Female Advocacy Project is certain to be dealt a serious blow by the policies of the Reagan administration and by an associated political climate hostile to the advance of groups lacking power in the society; notably, low-income groups, women, and children. Drastic cuts in human welfare programs will swell the juvenile offender population while the governmental apparatus for redress and relief is simultaneously being dismantled.

The architects of the National Female Advocacy Project were not unaware of these familiar cyclic swings in our national life;

their effort is to build a movement for young women strong enough to ride out the hurricane. Whether or not that nascent movement will become, as the project hopes, ''a lasting feature of society'' remains to be seen.

Notes

Listen to Me: A Female Status Offender's Story

1. *Are My Dreams Too Much to Ask For?*, edited by Debby Rosenberg and Carol Zimmerman (Tucson, Ariz.: New Directions for Young Women, 1977), p. 89. The bulk of Carol Warren's interview, from which her story as presented in this article is drawn, appears on pp. 111-117. "Carol Warren" is a pseudonym.

2. *Removing Children from Adult Jails: A Guide to Action* (Community Research Forum, University of Illinois at Urbana-Champaign, prepared for United States Department of Justice, Law Enforcement Assistance Administration, Office of Juvenile Justice and Delinquency Prevention, May 1980), p. 1.

3. U.S. President's Commission on Law Enforcement and Administration of Justice, Task Force Report: Juvenile Delinquency and Youth Crime 4 (1967), cited in R. Hale Andrews, Jr., and Andrew H. Cohn, "Ungovernability: The Unjustifiable Jurisdiction," *The Yale Law Jouranl* 83:7 (June 1974), p. 1383.

4. Senator Birch Bayh, "Girls in Trouble: 'Second Class Delinquents,'" in *The Woman Offender Report* 1:1 (March/April 1975), pp. 6-7. For additional, similar national figures, see Female Offender Resource Center, *Little Sisters and the Law* (Washington, D.C.: United States Department of Justice, 1977), p. 1; Rosemary Sarri, "Juvenile Law: How It Penalizes Females," in *The Female Offender,* edited by Laura Crites (Lexington, Mass.: Lexington Books, 1976), p. 71.

For comparable figures in Minnesota, see Peter Rode and Lee Ann Osbun, with Frederick Grittner and Michael Robin, "Juvenile Court Intervention in Status Offense Cases: An Analysis of Current Practices in Minnesota" (Supreme Court Juvenile Justice Study Commission, February 1981). For New York State figures, see Andrews and Cohn, pp. 1386-1387.

5. John M. Rector, "The Challenge of Our Unjust Juvenile Justice System," in *Teenage Women in the Juvenile Justice System: Changing Values,* edited by Ruth Crow and Ginny McCarthy (Tucson, Ariz.: New Directions for Young Women, 1979), p. 52. Mr. Rector was administrator for the Office of Juvenile Justice and Delinquency Prevention of the LEAA under President Carter.

6. For parental referrals of children of both sexes, see Orman W. Ketcham, "Why Jurisdiction Over Status Offenders Should Be Eliminated from Juvenile Courts," *Boston University Law Review* 57:4 (July 1977), p. 649. For referral of girls to court by parents, see Susan K. Datesman and Frank R. Scarpitti, "Female Delinquency and Broken Homes: A Reassessment," *Criminology* (May 1975), pp. 33-56; Peter C. Kratcoski, "Differential Treatment of Delinquent Boys and Girls in Juvenile Court," *Child Welfare* 52:1 (January 1974), pp. 17-18; Andrews and Cohn, p. 1385, note

21; p. 1387, note 26.

7. From 1969 to 1975, a mere 5 percent of all federal juvenile justice funds were earmarked for females; the local expenditure of juvenile justice funds on girls' programs was only 6 percent. Law Enforcement Assistance Administration, *The Report of the LEAA Task Force on Women,* October 1, 1975, p. 10. A 1976 report on United Way allocations revealed that girls' organizations received one dollar out of every four donated to youth agencies by corporate foundations. Girls Clubs of America, Inc., broadside, "Agencies Serving Girls Can No Longer Operate Efficiently with a Stove, a Sewing Machine and a Loving Heart."

8. *Little Sisters and the Law,* p. 12; and Sarri, p. 77.

9. For disparities between the sexes in court referrals for sexual activity, see Andrews and Cohn, p. 1389, note 41, cont'd. For data derived from self-reports, see Patricia Y. Miller, "Gender, Delinquency, and Social Control," unpublished manuscript in review, 1977, p. 9. Quoted in Sandra M. Stehno and Thomas M. Young, "Young Women and the Juvenile Justice System: An Examination of National Data and Summaries of Fourteen Alternative Programs" (National Center for the Assessment of Alternatives to Juvenile Justice Processing, School of Social Service Administration, University of Chicago, February 1980), p. 13. Stehno and Young offer an exhaustive listing of self-report studies, including studies that compare self-report data and arrest data. The studies they reviewed are cited in full on pp. 82–84, notes 7–10.

Domestication as Reform: A Study of the Socialization of Wayward Girls, 1856-1905

1. Bradford K. Peirce, 2AR, Public Document 16, 1857, p. 26.

2. Barbara Welter, "The Cult of True Womanhood," *American Quarterly* (1966), pp. 151-174. In this article the author delineates the four qualities considered necessary for the ideal antebellum woman: domesticity, submission, purity, and piety. It is obvious that even in postbellum America, Lancaster's founders were very much influenced by this ideology.

3. Christopher Lasch, *Haven in a Heartless World: The Family Besieged* (New York: Basic Books, 1977).

4. For a comprehensive example of this work, see Michael B. Katz, *The People of Hamilton, Canada West* (Cambridge, Mass.: Harvard University Press, 1975); and Peter Laslett, *The World We Have Lost* (New York: Scribner, 1965).

5. The Fay Commission, headed by Francis Fay, a legislator, was appointed by the Massachusetts Legislature in 1854 specifically to begin plans for a state reform school for girls.

6. For a more detailed description of this movement, see Michel Foucault, *The Birth of the Clinic* (New York: Pantheon, 1973); Michel Foucault, *Discipline and Punish* (New York: Pantheon, 1977); Gerald N. Grob, *The State and the Mentally Ill* (Chapel Hill: University of North Carolina Press, 1965); Gerald N. Grob, *Mental Institutions in America*

(New York: Free Press, 1973); David W. Lewis, *From Newgate to Danne-mora* (Ithaca: Cornell University Press, 1965); Barbara Gutman, *Public Health and the State* (Cambridge, Mass.: Harvard University Press, 1972); David Rothman, *The Discovery of the Asylum* (Boston: Little, Brown, 1971).

7. Lawrence A. Cremin, *The Republic and the School: Horace Mann on the Education of Free Men* (New York: Teachers College Press, 1957), p. 33.

8. Michael B. Katz, *The Irony of Early School Reform* (Cambridge, Mass.: Harvard University Press, 1968), pp. 163–211.

9. Douglas E. Branch, *The Sentimental Years* (New York: Hill & Wang, 1965), pp. 289–318.

10. "Commissioner's Report," Massachusetts House Document 43, 1854, p. 6.

11. "Commissioner's Report," p. 34.

12. "An Act," Massachusetts House Document 43, 1854, p. 51.

13. *John Stuart Mill on Bentham and Coleridge,* edited by F.R. Leavis (New York: Harper & Row, 1950).

14. "First Annual Report of the Superintendent and Chaplain," Massachusetts *1AR* House Document 20, 1856, p. 35.

15. Oscar Handlin, *Boston's Immigrants* (New York: Atheneum, 1972); Malwyn A. Jones, *American Immigration* (Chicago: University of Chicago Press, 1960); U.S. Dept. of Commerce, Bureau of the Census, *Historical Statistics of the United States: Colonial Times to 1970,* pp. 87–121.

16. *The Educating of Americans: A Documentary History,* edited by Daniel Calhoun (Boston: Houghton Mifflin, 1969), pp. 158–171; Carl F. Kaestle, *The Evolution of an Urban School System: New York City, 1750–1850* (Cambridge, Mass.: Harvard University Press, 1973), pp. 148–158.

17. By using the occupational ranking scheme devised by Michael B. Katz in *The People of Hamilton, Canada West,* pp. 343–348, I was able to assess the fathers' occupational rank. The number of fathers who were dead, had deserted, or whose occupation was "uncategorized" showed that the girls at Lancaster were from extremely poor homes. Those mothers who worked held exceptionally low-ranked jobs.

18. I calculated Irish or Irish-American girls as Catholics when the reli-gion of the girls was not explicitly stated.

19. Massachusetts 2AR, Public Document 16, 1856, p. 14.

20. Massachusetts 2AR, House Document, 1857, p. 10.

21. Bradford K. Peirce, *First Handwritten Casebook,* 1856, p. 1.

22. Pierce, *Casebook,* p. 1.

23. Porter N. Brown, *Handwritten Casebook,* 1880. Case 1062.

24. Brown, Case 1070.

25. Mrs. L. Brackett, *Handwritten Casebook,* 1890, Case 1557.

26. Mrs. L. Brackett, *Handwritten Casebook,* 1905, Case 2751.

27. The following three acts brought about de facto classification. Sects. 8 and 10, Chap 359, Acts of 1870, allowed the Visiting Agent of the Board of State Charities to attend trials and to oversee placement once the

girls received their sentences. At the same time, Chap. 365, Acts of 1871, gave the Board the power of transfer of girls to Lancaster from other institutions. It also sanctioned the commitment of seventeen-year-olds to Lancaster.

28. Until 1872 the Primary School was really an adjunct to the Monson Almshouse. In 1872 the Primary School became independent of the Almshouse, sharing its trusteeship with the two reform schools. The increasing bureaucratization of the State Board of Charities eroded the informal mechanisms the founders felt necessary to work with these children. Bitter controversies arose over the education program and placement at Monson. In addition, hardened criminal children were placed with young destitute children. In 1886 the State Primary School at Monson was opened for the purpose of housing destitute and deprived young children; it was considered a preferable alternative to the Almshouse or reform school. The Primary School suffered the same fate at Lancaster, however. The legislature closed the school in 1895.

29. Massachusetts 4AR, Public Document 24, 1859, p. 6.

30. Massachusetts *22AR,* to State Board of Health, Lunacy, and Charity, Public Document 20, 1877, p. 7.

31. Massachusetts, *22AR,* 1877, p. 14.

32. Massachusetts *32AR* to the State Board of Lunacy and Charity, Public Document 18, 1887, p. 14.

33. Massachusetts *13AR,* to the Board of State Charities, Public Document 20, 1868, p. 2.

34. Massachusetts *13AR,* 1868, p. 2.

35. Massachusetts *13AR,* 1868, p. 8.

36. Massachusetts *19AR* to the Board of State Charities, Public Document 20, 1874, p. 8.

37. David M. Katzman, *Seven Days a Week* (Oxford: Oxford University Press, 1978).

38. Barbara Brenzel and Walter McCann, "Education Technical," *Encyclopedia of Sociology* (Guilford, Conn.: Dushkin Press, 1974). For a more detailed and comprehensive account see Marvin Lazerson, *The Origins of the Urban Public School* (Cambridge, Mass.: Harvard University Press, 1971); and *American Education and Vocationalism,* edited by Marvin Lazerson and W. Norton Grubb (New York: Teachers College Press, 1974).

39. Stephan Thernstrom, *The Other Bostonians* (Cambridge, Mass.: Harvard University Press, 1973), pp. 45–75; Stephan Thernstrom, *Poverty and Progress* (Cambridge, Mass.: Harvard University Press, 1964), pp. 150–152. Thernstrom describes static families. The girls are Lancaster seem to come from families like the ones Thernstrom describes as "unable to rise out of the most depressed impoverished segment of the manual laboring class."

40. Carol Peacock, "The Massachusetts Experiment: Towards Equal Services for Girls" (Boston: Department of Youth Services, 1978). I have also benefited from numerous conversations with Claire Donovan, former Superintendent of State Industrial School, Lancaster.

From Benign Neglect to Malign Attention: A Critical Review of Recent Research on Female Delinquency

1. Travis Hirschi, *Causes of Delinquency* (Berkeley: University of California Press, 1969), pp. 35–36.

2. Albert K. Cohen, *Delinquent Boys* (Glencoe, Illinois: The Free Press, 1955). Similar assumptions can be found in more recent works as well. See Ira J. Silverman and Simon Dinitz, "Compulsive Masculinity and Delinquency," *Criminology* 11 (February 1974), pp. 498–515.

3. Frances Heidensohn, "The Deviance of Women: A Critique and an Enquiry," *British Journal of Sociology* 11 (June 1968), pp. 160–176.

4. Two of the best known of the books which attempted to establish a link between the rising arrest rates of women and the women's liberation movement are Freda Adler's *Sisters in Crime* (New York: McGraw-Hill, 1975) and Richard Deming's *Women: The New Criminals* (New York: Dell Publishing Co., 1977).

5. The ubiquity of female subservience has traditionally encouraged men to trivialize or overlook actual female defiance, particularly so long as it does not directly challenge the bedrock of female oppression (woman's status as male sexual property). Because of this, when women do organize to demand some semblance of equality, their movements tend to avoid overt criticism of the female role and instead address less sensitive issues such as suffrage and economic equity. Typically, these demands are met first with humor, and next with the argument that their realization would contaminate women and thus render them incapable of fulfilling their sacred obligations as wife and mother.

One largely ignored component of this position is the idea that the woman who rejects her "place" and seeks equality with men is clearly flirting with vicious criminality. One of the earliest commentators on female criminality, Cesare Lombroso (*The Female Offender.* New York: Philosophical Library., 1958, p. 151), made this connection quite clearly:

> We have seen that women have many traits in common with children; that their moral sense is deficient; that they are revengeful, jealous, inclined to vengeances of refined cruelty. In ordinary cases these defects are neutralized by piety, maternity, want of passion, sexual coldness, by neatness and an undeveloped intelligence. But when a morbid activity of the physical centres intensifies the bad qualities of women, and induces them to seek relief in evil deeds; when piety and maternal sentiments are wanting, and in their place are strong passions and intensely erotic tendencies, much muscular strength and a superior intelligence for the conception and execution of evil, it is clear that the innocuous demi-criminal present in the normal woman must be transformed into a born criminal more terrible than any man.

This bald misogynist logic has over the years been refined to the thesis that even minimal recognition of rights for women will result in a dramatic increase in female participation in crime.

6. Federal Bureau of Investigation, *Uniform Crime Reports* (Washing-

ton, D.C.: U.S. Department of Justice, 1976).

7. Joseph G. Weis, "Liberation and Crime: The Invention of the New Female Criminal," *Crime and Social Justice* 6 (1976), p. 17.

8. *Honolulu Star-Bulletin,* "L.A. Police Chief Blames Libbers," August 7, 1975.

9. Steven Roberts, "Crime Rate of Women Up Sharply Over Men's," *New York Times* June 13, 1971, pp. 1–3.

10. Adler, p. 3.

11. Darrell J. Steffensmeier, "Sex Differences in Patterns of Adult Crime, 1965–77: A Review and Assessment," *Social Forces* 58:4 (June 1980).

12. *Ibid.,* p. 1080.

13. Darrell J. Steffensmeier and Renee Hoffman Steffensmeier, "Trends in Femal Delinquency," *Criminology* 18:1 (1980).

14. *Ibid.,* p. 65. It should be noted here that suspicion is not an offense, but it is a ground for many arrests in those jurisdictions where the law permits. This category comprises those individuals who were arrested but subsequently released without charges. U.S. Department of Justice, *Sourcebook of Criminal Justice Statistics, 1980* (Washington, D.C.: Criminal Justice Research Center, 1981), p. 581.

15. Steffensmeier and Steffensmeier, p. 72.

16. Weis, p. 23.

17. *Ibid.,* p. 24.

18. Martin Gold and David J. Reimer, "Changing Patterns of Delinquent Behavior Among Americans 13 through 16 Years Old: 1967-72," *Crime and Delinquency Literature* 7 (December 1975), p. 492.

19. Steffensmeier and Steffensmeier, p. 79.

20. Jennifer James and William Thornton, "Women's Liberation and the Female Delinquent," *Journal of Research in Crime and Delinquency* 17:2 (July 1980).

21. *Ibid.,* p. 243.

22. Stephen Norland, Randall C. Wessell, and Neal Shover, "Masculinity and Delinquency," *Criminology* 19:3 (November 1981), pp. 421–433.

23. Joseph H. Rankin, "School Factors and Delinquency: Interactions by Age and Sex," *Sociology and Social Research* 64:3 (1980), pp. 420–434.

24. See Susan K. Datesman, Frank R. Scarpitti, and Richard M. Stephenson, "Female Delinquency: An Application of Self and Opportunity Theories," *Journal of Research in Crime and Delinquency* (July 1975), pp. 107–122; Gary J. Jensen and Raymond Eve, "Sex Differences in Delinquency," *Criminology* 13 (February 1976), pp. 427–448; Neal Shover, Steven Norland, Jennifer James and William Thornton, "Gender Roles and Delinquency," *Social Forces* 58 (September 1979), pp. 162–175; Neal Shover and Stephen Norland, "Sex Roles and Criminality: Science of Conventional Wisdom," *Sex Roles* 4 (January 1978), pp. 111–125; Ronald L. Simons, Martin H. Miller, and Stephen M. Aigner, "Contemporary Theories of Deviance and Female Delinquency: An Empirical Test," *Journal of Research in Crime and Delinquency* 17:1 (January 1980).

25. Law Enforcement Assistance Administration, *The Report of the LEAA Task Force on Women,* October 1, 1975, p. 10.

26. Female Offender Resource Center, *Little Sisters and the Law* (Washington, D.C.: United States Department of Justice, 1977), pp. 14–19.

27. *Ibid.,* pp. 16–19.

28. Maurice J. Boisvert and Robert Wells, "Toward a Rational Policy on Status Offenders," *Social Work* 25:3 (May 1980), p. 233.

29. See Marianne Felice and David Offord, "Girl Delinquency . . . A Review," *Corrective Psychiatry and Journal of Social Therapy* 17(2), pp. 18–28, for a thorough review of literature on the characteristics of female delinquents. For information on the role that sexual abuse plays in the creation of female delinquency, see National Institute of Mental Health, *Study of Females in Detention* (King County, Washington, 1977), which gave figures of 40–50 percent physical and/or sexual abuse, 17 percent subjected to incest among girls in detention.

30. Otto Pollak, *The Criminality of Women* (Philadelphia: University of Pennsylvania, 1950), p. 151.

31. The development of the chivalry theory is well documented in Etta Anderson, "The Chivalrous Treatment of the Female Offender in the Arms of the Criminal Justice System: A Review of the Literature," *Social Problems* 23 (1976), pp. 349–57.

32. Ruth S. Cavan, *Criminology* (New York: Crowell, 1962), p. 32.

33. John Cowie, Valerie Cowie, and Eliot Slater, *Delinquency in Girls* (Chicago: Aldine Press, 1968), p. 1.

34. J.D. Acheson and D.C. Williams, "A Study of Juvenile Sex Offenders," *American Journal of Psychiatry* 3 (1954), p. 370.

35. P. Blos, *On Adolescence: A Psycho-Analytic Interpretation* (New York: The Free Press, 1962).

36. Clyde B. Vedder and Dora B. Somerville, *The Delinquent Girl* (Springfield, Ill.: Charles C. Thomas, 1970), p. viii.

37. The silence on the discriminatory treatment of women was broken almost simultaneously by women from many parts of the country. What follows is a listing of the earliest published pieces. Meda Chesney-Lind, "Judicial Enforcement of the Female Sex Role: The Family Court and the Female Delinquent," *Issues in Criminology* 8 (Fall, 1973), pp. 51–70; Sarah Gold, "Equal Protection for Juvenile Girls in Need of Supervision in New York State," *New York Law Forum* 17 (1971), pp. 570-598; Kristine Rogers, "For Her Own Protection," *Law and Society* 7 (1972), pp. 223–246; Florence Rush, "The Myth of Sexual Delinquency," *Women: A Journal of Liberation* 3 (1973), pp. 38–40; Jean Strousse, "To Be Minor and Female," *Ms* (August 1972), pp. 70–75.

38. See Weis, pp. 17-27.

39. Chesney-Lind, pp. 51–70.

40. See R. Hale Andrews, Jr., and Andrew H. Cohn, "Ungovernability: The Unjustifiable Jurisdiction," *The Yale Law Journal* 83:7 (June 1974), pp. 1383-1409; and Martin Kohn and Norman Sugarman, "Characteristics of Families Coming to the Family Court on PINS Petitions,"

Psychiatric Quarterly 50:1 (1978), pp. 37–43.

41. Susan Datesman and Frank Scarpitti, "Unequal Protection for Males and Females in the Juvenile Court," in *Juvenile Delinquency,* edited by Theodore N. Ferdinand (Beverly Hills: Sage Publications, 1977), pp. 59–77.

42. Richard H. Chused, "The Juvenile Court Process: A Study of Three New Jersey Counties," *Rutger's Law Review* 26:2 (Winter 1973), pp. 488–589.

43. P.C. Kratcoski, "Differential Treatment of Boys and Girls by the Juvenile Justice System," *Child Welfare* 53 (January 1974), pp. 16–22.

44. See Al Katz and Lee H. Teitelbaum,"PINS Jurisdiction, the Vagueness Doctrine and the Rule of Law," in *Beyond Control: Status Offenders in the Juvenile Court,* edited by Lee H. Teitelbaum and Aidan R. Gough (Cambridge, Mass.: Ballinger, 1977); Orman W. Ketchum, "Why Jurisdiction over Status Offenders should be Removed from the Juvenile Court," in *Status Offenders and the Juvenile Justice System* (Hackensack, New Jersey: National Council on Crime and Delinquency, 1978); Nicholas N. Kittrie, *The Right to Be Different* (Baltimore: Penguin Books, 1973); and Rosemary Sarri, "Juvenile Law: How it Penalizes Females," in *The Female Offender,* edited by Laura Crites (Lexington, Mass.: Lexington Books, 1976).

45. Strouse, pp. 70–75.

46. Steven Schlossman and Stephanie Wallach, "The Crime of Precocious Sexuality: Female Juvenile Delinquency in the Progressive Era," *Harvard Educational Review* 48 (February 1978), p. 67.

47. Alan Sussman, "Sex-Based Discrimination and the PINS Jurisdiction," in Teitelbaum and Gough, pp. 179–199.

48. Lesley Shacklady Smith, "Sexist Assumptions and Female Delinquency," in *Women, Sexuality and Social Control,* edited by Carol Smart and Barry Smart (London: Routledge, 1978), p. 83.

49. Chesney-Lind, pp. 51–70.

50. Strouse, pp. 70–75; Lois Forer, *No One Will Lissen* (New York: John Day and Co., 1970); Loretta Schwartz, "The Kid Nobody Wants," paper distributed by the Philadelphia Program for Women and Girl Offenders; Randall Shelden, "Sex Discrimination in the Juvenile Justice System: A Case Study of Memphis, Tennessee, 1900–1917," paper presented at the American Society of Criminology Meetings, 1980; and Edward Wakin, *Children Without Justice: A Report by the National Council of Jewish Women* (New York: National Council of Jewish Women, 1975).

51. Datesman and Scarpitti, pp. 107–122.

52. *Ibid.,* p. 70.

53. Katherine S. Teilmann and Pierre H. Landry, Jr., "Gender Bias in Juvenile Justice," *Journal of Research in Crime and Delinquency* 18:1 (January 1981), pp. 47–80.

54. *Ibid.,* p. 47.

55. Stevens H. Clarke and Gary G. Koch, "Juvenile Court: Therapy on Crime Control, and Do Lawyers Make a Difference," *Law and Society Review* 14:2 (Winter 1980), pp. 263–308.

56. *Ibid.,* p. 287.

57. Teilmann and Landry, pp. 74–75.

58. Richard Flaste, "Is Juvenile Justice Tougher on Girls than Boys," *New York Times,* September 6, 1977.

59. Clarke and Koch, p. 287.

60. Teilmann and Landry, p. 67.

61. R. Hale Andrews, Jr., and Andrew H. Cohn, "PINS Processing in New York: An Evaluation," in Teitelbaum and Gough, p. 70; and Lawrence Cohen, *Delinquency Dispositions: An Empirical Analysis of Processing Decision in Three Juvenile Courts* (Washington, D.C.: U.S. Government Printing Office, 1975).

62. Andrews and Cohn, "PINS Processing," pp. 80–81.

63. Lawrence E. Cohen and James R. Kluegal, "Selecting Delinquents for Adjudication," *Journal of Research in Crime and Delinquency* (January 1979), pp. 143–163, and Lawrence E. Cohen and James R. Kluegal, "The Detention Decision: A Study of the Impact of Social Characteristics and Legal Factors in Two Metropolitan Courts," *Social Forces* 58 (September 1979).

64. Cohen and Kluegal, "Selecting Delinquents for Adjudication," p. 158.

65. Boisvert and Wells, p. 232.

66. Albert J. Reiss, "Sex Offenses: The Marginal Status of Adolescents," *Law and Contemporary Problems* 25 (1960), p. 316.

67. Linda Hancock, "The Myth That Females are Treated More Leniently than Males in the Juvenile Justice System," *Australian and New Zealand Journal of Sociology* 16:3 (November 1981), pp. 4–14.

68. Schlossman and Wallach, pp. 65-94.

69. Sheldon, p. 14.

70. Tony Hoffman, "Sex Discrimination in Oregon's Juvenile Justice System," paper presented at the Spring Meeting of the Oregon Psychological Association, Newport, Oregon, May, 1981.

71. U.S. Department of Justice, "Children in Custody Advance Report on the 1979 Census of Public Juvenile Facilities" (Washington, D.C.: LEAA, 1980).

72. U.S. Department of Justice, "Children in Custody: Advance Report on the 1979 Census of Private Juvenile Facilities" (Washington, D.C.: LEAA, 1981). In the period between 1977–79, the number of males in private custody increased slightly, 1977 and 1979, while the number of females continued to decline.

73. The clearest example of the New Right's attempt to re-empower the traditional family is the "Moral Majority's" Rev. Jerry Falwell's "Ninety-Five Theses for the 1980s," which, among other things, suggest that "God himself has instituted marriage," that "the husband is looked upon as the divinely appointed head of this institution," and that "children belong to the parents and are not wards of the state." Consistent with this "pro-family" orientation, the "Family Protection Act of 1981" has been submitted to Congress by Roger Jepsen (R-Iowa) and Paul Laxalt (R-Nevada) in the Senate and Albert Lee Smith (R-Alabama) in the House.

This act, which has been "designed to strengthen the American family," has six titles which would provide for a "legal presumption in favor of an expansion interpretation" of the parental role in supervising and determining the religious or moral formation of the child. Among other things, it would prohibit the federal government from preempting or interfering with state statutes pertaining to juvenile delinquency, child abuse, or spouse abuse. The definition of child abuse would be revised to exclude corporal punishment or other forms of discipline "applied by a parent or individual explicitly authorized by a parent." Federal funding for child and spouse programs would also be restricted.

74. Despite the widespread impression that youthful crime, specifically violent youthful crime, has increased dramatically in recent years, data collected by the Justice Department and the Census Bureau in their surveys of crime victims do not support such a conclusion. These polls indicate that the annual rate of assaults, larcenies, robberies, and rapes committed by juveniles (12 to 17) fell 11.2 percent between 1973 and 1977. See Office of Juvenile Justice and Delinquency Prevention "Analysis of National Crime Victimization Survey Data to Study Serious Delinquent Behavior" (Washington, D.C.: U.S. Department of Justice, 1982), pp. 110–124.

Easy Money: Female Adolescent Involvement in Prostitution

1. J. James and J. Meyerding, "Early Sexual Experience as a Factor in Prostitution," *Archives of Sexual Behavior* 7:1 (1977), pp. 31–42.

2. Harold Greenwald, *The Elegant Prostitute* (New York: Ballantine Books, 1970). Also see Wardell Pomeroy, "Some Aspects of Prostitution," *Journal of Sex Research* (November 1965), pp. 177–87; Harry Benjamin and R.E.L. Masters, *Prostitution and Morality* (New York: Julien Press, 1964); T.C. Esselstyn, "Prostitution in the United States," *Annals of the American Academy of Political and Social Sciences* (March 1968), pp. 123–35; Kingsley Davis, "The Sociology of Prostitution," *American Sociological Review* 2 (1937), pp. 744–755.

3. Tage Kemp, *Prostitution: An Investigation of its Causes, Especially with Regard to Hereditary Factors* (Copenhagen: Levin & Muskgaard, 1937).

4. Charles Winick and Paul M. Kinsie, *The Lively Commerce* (New York: New American Library, 1971), p. 75. See also Greenwald, p. 202.

5. Diana Gray, "Turning Out: A Study of Teenage Prostitution," *Urban Life and Culture* 1 (1973), pp. 401–24. Also see Pomeroy, p. 184; Kemp, p. 190; Benjamin and Masters, p.107.

6. Maryse Choisy, *Psychoanalysis of the Prostitute* (New York: Philosophical Library, 1961). Also see Arnold S. Maerov, "Prostitution: A Survey & Review of 20 Cases," *The Pate Report* (1965), pp. 675–701; Norman R. Jackman, Richard O'Toole and Gilbert Geis, "The Self-Image of the Prostitute," in *Sexual Deviance,* edited by John H. Gagnon and William Simon (New York: Harper & Row, 1967), pp. 133–146; Nanette Davis, "The Prostitute: Developing a Deviant Identity," in *Studies in the Sociol-*

ogy of Sex, edited by J. Henslin (New York: Appleton-Century-Crofts, 1971).

7. D.E. Carnes, "Talking About Sex: Notes on First Coitus and the Double Sex Standard," *Journal of Marriage and the Family* 35 (1973), pp. 677–88. Also see Vincent DeFrancis, "Protecting the Child Victim of Sex Crimes by Adults," *Federal Probation* (September 1971), pp. 15–20; and James and Meyerding, pp. 40–41.

8. Karen E. Rosenblum, "Female Deviance and the Female Sex Role: A Preliminary Investigation," *British Journal of Sociology* 26 (1975), pp. 169–85. Also see J.H. Bryan, "Apprenticeships in Prostitution," in Gagnon and Simon, pp. 146–164.

9. Marshall Clinard, *Sociology of Deviant Behavior* (New York: Rinehart & Co., 1959). Also see Esselstyn, pp. 123–35.

10. Marc H. Hollender, "Prostitution, the Body and Human Relatedness," *International Journal of Psychoanalysis* 42 (1961), pp. 404–13, Also see Maerov, p. 686.

11. Greenwald, p. 194.

12. Choisy, *passim.*

13. Maerov, pp. 695; 696.

14. Greenwald, p. 198; Winick and Kinsie, pp. 84–88.

15. Clyde Vedder and Dora Sommerville, *The Delinquent Girl* (Springfield, Ill.: Charles C. Thomas, 1970). Also see Valeris Cowie and Eliot Slater, *Delinquency in Girls* (London: Heinemann, 1968).

16. See, for example, Florence Rush, "The Myth of Sexual Delinquency," *Androgyny* 3 (1976), pp. 89–90; T.C.N. Gibbens, "Juvenile Prostitution," *British Journal of Delinquency* 3 (1957), pp. 3–12.

17. Federal Bureau of Investigation, *Uniform Crime Reports* (Washington, D.C.: U.S. Department of Justice, 1978). Total arrests for juvenile prostitutes under eighteen were as follows:

	1969	1974	1978
Male	236	754	891
Female	617	1,573	2,031

18. Gray, pp. 401–24.

19. Nancy B. Greene and T.C. Esselstyn, "The Beyond Control Girl," *Juvenile Justice* 23 (1972), pp. 13–19. Also see Meda Chesney-Lind, "Judicial Enforcement of the Female Sex Role: The Family and Court and the Female Delinquent," *Issues in Criminology* 8 (1973), pp. 51–69. Also see Don C. Gibbons, *Delinquent Behavior* (Englewood Cliffs, New Jersey: Prentice Hall, Inc., 1970).

20. Carole Upshur, "Delinquency in Girls: Implications for Service Delivery," in *Closing Correctional Institutions,* edited by Yitzak Bakal (Lexington, Mass.: Lexington Books, 1973).

21. *Family Dynamics and Female Sexual Delinquency,* edited by O. Pollak and A. Friedman (Palo Alto, Calif.: Science and Behavior Books, 1969).

22. M. Felice and D.R. Offord, "Three Developmental Pathways to Delinquency in Girls," *British Journal of Criminology* 12:4 (1972), pp. 375–389.

23. Gisela Konopka, *The Adolescent Girl in Conflict* (Englewood Cliffs, New Jersey: Prentice Hall, 1966), pp. 38–45; 70–86. Also see Mary Gray Reige, "Parental Affection and Juvenile Delinquency in Girls," *British Journal of Criminology and Deviant Social Behavior* 12 (1972), pp. 55–73.

24. Albert Reiss, "Sex Offenses of Adolescents," in *Readings in Juvenile Delinquency,* edited by Ruth Cavan (Philadelphia, Penn.: Lippincott, 1964), pp. 268–72. Also see Marie Bertrand, "Self-Image and Delinquency," *Acta Criminologica* 2 (1969), pp. 71–144; and David M. Connell, "Relationship Between Sex-Role Identity and Self-Esteem in Early Adolescents," *Developmental Psychology* 3 (1970), p. 268.

25. Herbert H. Hersovitz, "A Psychodynamic View of Sexual Promiscuity," in Pollak and Friedman, pp. 89–99. Also see in Pollak and Friedman: Ames Robey, "The Runaway Girl," pp. 127–137; Peter Blos, "Three Typical Constellations in Female Delinquency," pp. 99–111; and N.W. Ackerman, "Sexual Delinquency among Middle-Class Girls," pp. 45–51.

26. Konopka, pp. 96–98; Reige, pp. 71–72.

27. For this approach, see, for example, Konopka; Reige; and Pollack and Friedman.

28. H. Kagan, *Prostitution and Sexual Promiscuity among Adolescent Female Offenders* (Ann Arbor, Mich.: University Microfilms International, 1969), pp. 401–24.

29. A.R. Harris, "Sex and Theories of Deviance: Toward a Functional Theory of Deviant Type Scripts," *American Sociological Review* 42:1 (1977), pp. 3–16.

30. P. Miller, "Delinquency and Gender," unpublished manuscript (State of Illinois Institute for Juvenile Research, 1978). Also see Nanette Davis, "Feminism, Deviance and Social Change," in *Deviance and Social Change,* edited by E. Sagarin (Beverly Hills, Calif.: Sage Publications, 1977). Also see Rosenblum, pp. 169–85.

31. Rosenblum, p. 169.

32. N. Davis, p. 299.

33. Jennifer James and Peter Vitaliano, "Multivariate Analysis of Entrance into Prostitution," in Proceedings of the Third International Congress of Medical Sexology, edited by R. Forleo and W. Pasini (Rome, Italy, 1979).

34. James and Meyerding, pp. 40–41.

35. Jennifer James, Principal Investigator, "Entrance into Juvenile Prostitution" (Department of Psychiatry and Behavioral Sciences, University of Washington, Seattle, funded by Grant #R01 MH 29968, Public Health Service, National Institute of Mental Health, August 1980).

36. FBI, *Uniform Crime Reports,* 1978.

37. "Juvenile Prostitution: A Federal Strategy for Combatting Its Causes and Consequences," submitted to the Youth Development Bureau, Office of Human Development, HEW, 1978.

38. Jennifer James, "Motivations for Entrance into Prostitution," in *The Female Offender,* edited by Laura Crites (Lexington, Mass.: Lexington Books, 1976), pp. 177–205.

39. James, "Entrance into Juvenile Prostitution."

40. James and Meyerding, p. 38.

41. Jennifer James, Principal Investigator, "Female Criminal Involvement and Narcotics Addiction" (Department of Psychiatry and Behavioral Sciences, University of Washington, Seattle, funded 1974–1977 by Grant #R01 DA 00918, Public Health Service, Division of Research, National Institute on Drug Abuse, August 1977).

42. F. Ferracuti, "Incest Between Father and Daugher," in *Sexual Behaviors: Social Clinical and Legal Aspects,* edited by H.L. Resnik and M.E. Wolfgang (Boston: Little, Brown, 1972). Also see I.B. Weiner, "Father–Daughter Incest: A Clinical Report," *Psychology Quarterly* 36 (1962), pp. 607–32.

43. J. Gagnon, "Female Child Victims of Sex Offenses," *Social Problems* 13 (1965), pp. 176–192.

44. DeFrancis, pp. 15–20.

45. James and Meyerding, pp. 31–42.

46. *Ibid.*

47. Report from Zero Population Growth (1346 Connecticut Avenue, N.W., Washington, D.C. 20036, August 1977). One in 10 adolescent females ages 15–19 becomes pregnant; of those who become pregnant, 6 in 10 result in live births, 3 in 10 are aborted, 1 in 10 miscarry.

48. David Finkelhor, *Sexually Victimized Children* (New York: The Free Press/Macmillan, 1979). The author states that 1 in 11 boys are sexually abused prior to age eighteen.

49. David Matza, *Delinquency and Drift* (New York: John Wiley and Sons, 1964), p. 28.

50. *Ibid.*

51. *Ibid.,* p. 29.

52. Jennifer James and Peter Vitaliano, *Drift Towards Sex Role Deviance,* ERIC Reports (Arlington, Virginia: Microfilm Publication, 1978).

53. N. Davis, p. 299.

54. *Ibid.*

55. Jennifer James and Peter Vitaliano, *Drift Towards Sex Role Deviance,* p. 2.

56. *Ibid.,* pp. 17–18.

57. E. Lemert, *Human Deviance, Social Problems and Social Control* (Englewood Cliffs, New Jersey: Prentice Hall, 1972).

58. Rosenblum, p. 169.

59. *Ibid.,* p. 177.

60. *Ibid.,* p. 182.

61. Matza, *Delinquency and Drift,* and Matza, *Becoming Deviant* (Englewood Cliffs, New Jersey: Prentice-Hall, Inc., 1969).

62. James and Vitaliano, *Drift Towards Sex Role Deviance,* p. 8; James and Meyerding, pp. 40–41; N. Davis, pp. 301–02.

63. N. Davis, p. 299.

64. Matza, *Becoming Deviant,* p. 198.

65. N. Davis, p. 321.

66. Rosenblum, pp. 169–85.

67. Peter Vitaliano, Jennifer James and Debra Boyer, "Sexuality of Deviant Females: Adolescent and Adult Correlates," *Social Work* 26:6 (November 1981), pp. 468–472.

68. Matza, *Becoming Deviant*, p. 157.

69. N. Davis, p. 305.

70. Rosenblum, p. 180.

71. Matza, *Becoming Deviant*, p. 170.

72. *Ibid.*, p. 142.

73. N. Davis, p. 311.

74. Matza, *Delinquency and Drift*, p. 22.

75. Roberta Simmons, Dale Blythe, Edward F. VanCleave and Diane Bush, "Entry into Early Adolescence: The Impact of School Structure, Puberty, and Early Dating on Self-Esteem," *American Sociological Review* 44 (December 1979), p. 948.

76. N. Davis, pp. 315–318.

77. A Bandura, "The Self-System in Reciprocal Determinism," *American Psychologist* 33 (1978), pp. 344–358.

78. Peter Vitaliano, Debra Boyer and Jennifer James, "Perceptions of Juvenile Experience Among Females Involved in Prostitution versus Property Offenses," *Criminal Justice and Behavior* 8:3 (September 1981), pp. 325–42.

79. Vitaliano, James and Boyer, "Sexuality of Deviant Females," p. 471. Also see Debra Boyer and Jennifer James, "Counseling Juvenile Female Prostitutes," unpublished paper (Department of Psychiatry and Behavioral Sciences, University of Washington, Seattle, funded by Grant #R01 MH 29968, Public Health Service, National Institute of Mental Health).

The Politics of Sexual Assault: Facing the Challenge

1. Mimi H. Silbert, Principal Investigator, "Sexual Assault of Prostitutes" (Delancy Street Foundation, 2563 Divisadero, San Francisco, Calif. 94115), November 1980.

2. See Judith Herman, *Father–Daughter Incest* (Cambridge, Mass.: Harvard University Press, 1981); David Finkelhor, *Sexually Victimized Children* (New York: Free Press, 1979); Florence Rush, *The Best Kept Secret* (Englewood Cliffs, N.J.: Prentice-Hall, 1980).

3. Rush, pp. 80–104; Herman, pp. 9–11.

4. Herman, pp. 16–18.

5. Sandra Butler, "The Tyranny of Theory," *Aegis* (Summer 1980), pp. 48–55.

6. The Sexual Assault Center, Harborview Medical Center, 325 Ninth Ave., Seattle, Wash. 98104. For articles reflecting the center's approach, see Lucy Berliner, "Advocating for Sexually Abused Children in the Criminal Justice System," *Response* (December 1976), and "Child Sexual Abuse: What Happens Next?" *Victimology: An International Journal* (Summer 1977).

Child Assault Prevention Project, Women Against Rape, Columbus, Ohio 43101. A teachers' guide and curriculum is scheduled for publication by CAP in 1982.

7. Pam Allan, *Free Space: A Perspective on the Small Group in Women's Liberation* (New York: Times Change Press, 1970).

Advocacy for Teenage Women in the Justice System: One Model for Change

1. Six hundred thousand youths are held annually in juvenile detention facilities; another 500,000 are held for one or more days in adult jails. Testimony presented at hearings of U.S. Subcommittee to Investigate Juvenile Delinquency, September 1973. For a similar, 1980 report, see *supra,* "Listen to Me," note 2.

On the ethnic and class backgrounds of juvenile court populations from the mid-nineteenth century to present times, see Anthony M. Platt, *The Child Savers: The Invention of Delinquency* (Chicago: The University of Chicago Press, 1977), pp. 139, 170–180, 189–192. On the over-representation of racial minorities in the juvenile justice system, see Orman W. Ketcham, "Why Jurisdiction over Status Offenders Should Be Eliminated from Juvenile Courts," *Boston University Law Review* 57:4 (July 1977), p. 658; and William Feyerherm, "Juvenile Court Dispositions of Status Offenders: An Analysis of Case Decision," in *Race, Crime, and Criminal Justice,* edited by R.L. McNeely and Carl E. Pope (Beverly Hills, Calif.: Sage Publications, 1981), pp. 134–139.

2. For a convenient, well-documented overview on status offenders in general and females in particular, see *Young Women and the Justice System: Basic Facts and Issues* (Tucson, Ariz.: New Directions for Young Women, 1981).

3. Rosemary Sarri and Robert Vinter, "Juvenile Justice and Injustice," *Resolution 1* (Winter 1975), p. 47. Also see sources given in this volume, "Listen to Me," note 4.

4. The grant was made and is administered by the Office of Juvenile Justice and Delinquency Prevention, created to implement the 1974 federal act.

5. "Juvenile Delinquency Prevention: A Compendium of Thirty-six Program Models" (Reports of the National Juvenile Justice Assessment Centers, prepared for U.S. Department of Justice, Law Enforcement Assistance Administration, Office of Juvenile Justice and Delinquency Prevention, 1980), pp. 79–80.

6. New Directions for Young Women employs a counseling staff of three full and two part-time workers.

7. The National Council of Jewish Women has a pre-history of special concern with the problems of youth. The council has published a general study of the juvenile justice system in the United States. See Edward Wakin, *Children without Justice: A Report by the National Council of Jewish Women* (New York: National Council of Jewish Women, 1975).

8. Memo to conference participants from Severa Austin, State of Wisconsin Department of Health and Social Services, dated September 17, 1980.

About the Contributors

Debra Boyer is a doctoral candidate in anthropology at the University of Washington. She currently works as a research analyst in the university's Department of Psychiatry and Behavioral Sciences. Her research with Jennifer James has been focussed on the relationships between female deviance and sex-role conflicts. Ms. Boyer has lectured and written on the topics of adolescent prostitution and sexuality and on female criminality and delinquency.

Barbara Brenzel is an assistant professor at Wellesley College and chairperson of its Department of Education. She is on leave in 1981-1982 as a Bunting Institute Fellow at the Schlesinger Library and a Radcliffe Research Scholar at the Henry A. Murray Center. After taking the B.A. in English at the University of Toronto, she was a high school teacher in that city for a number of years. She later earned a Ph.D. in the history of education from Harvard University. Her research on the history of institutions for girls is reflected in the publication of articles on that subject; and she is presently completing a book for M.I.T. Press titled *To Mend and Regenerate the Heart: A Social Portrait of the First Reform School for Girls in North America.*

Sandra Butler is the author of *Conspiracy of Silence: The Trauma of Incest.* Her work on the subject of sexual abuse of children originated in first-hand observation of clients while she was serving as director of the Sexual Trauma Center in San Francisco. She has lectured nationally on the subject and has done training and consulting with groups interested in problems of violence and sexual assault. Ms. Butler holds a master's degree in psychology and social systems from the San Francisco campus of Goddard College. Her works in progress include a novel and a book on the sexual abuse of women by their therapists.

Sue Davidson is information director of the National Female Advocacy Project of New Directions for Young Women. Between 1974-1980 she was an editor for The Feminist Press and a co-director of its *Women's Lives/Women's Work* project. She holds a master's degree in humanities from the University of Chicago and was a Fellow in Creative Writing at Stanford University. She is co-editor of *The Maimie Papers* and author of *What Do You Mean, Nonviolence?*, a booklet on alternatives to armed conflict. She has also published reportorial articles, fiction, and essays.

Jennifer James is an associate professor of psychiatry and behavioral sciences at the University of Washington and coordinator of research for the university's Division of Community Psychiatry. She took the M.A. in anthropology at Washington State University and the Ph.D. in anthropology at the University of Washington. Her research on the cultural basis of sex-role conflict and female deviance has led to the publication of numerous journal articles and the editing of two books on sexual victimization.

Meda Chesney-Lind is a sociologist with a long-standing interest in the situation of women within the criminal justice system. She received the M.A. and the Ph.D. in sociology from the University of Hawaii, where she is currently a researcher at the Youth Development and Research Center in the School of Social Work. She also teaches sociology at Honolulu Community College. She began her research on the treatment of female delinquents in the early 1970s, and has published articles on this subject in many scholarly and general journals. She is currently at work on a book titled *Delinquency in Girls.*

Debby Rosenberg holds a bachelor's degree in fine arts and a master's degree in education from the University of Arizona. She has been a teacher in the public schools of Tucson and a counselor at New Directions for Young Women, where she is presently program coordinator. She is co-editor of *Are My Dreams Too Much To Ask For?,* and is currently working on a manual on contemporary techniques in the counseling of young women.